BOMBER COMMAND

THE
THOUSAND
BOMBER
RAIDS

MARTYN CHORLTON

COUNTRYSIDE BOOKS
NEWBURY BERKSHIRE

COUNTRYSIDE BOOKS
3 Catherine Road
Newbury, Berkshire

To view our complete range of books,
Please visit us at
www.countrysidebooks.co.uk

ISBN 978 1 84674 347 4
Cover image by Piotr Forkasiewicz

Produced by The Letterworks Ltd., Reading
Typeset by KT Designs, St Helens
Printed by Short Run Press, Exeter

Contents

Acknowledgements

Firstly, I would like to thank Nick Battle and all the staff at Countryside Books for giving me the opportunity to produce a book on this fascinating and important subject. Special thanks to Alastair Goodrum for historical information and photographs and to John Clifford, curator of the excellent Pathfinder Museum also for historical documentation and photography. Thanks to Dr. Phil Judkins at the Purbeck Radar Museum and to Stuart Davidson of JD Transport Collectables for the chance to acquire many of the photographs in this book and help to build up a new archive on this subject. Thank you to Kelvin Youngs and his excellent website www.aircrewremembered.com and to Tony Buttler for various photographs and last but not least, to my wife Claire for proof reading my amateur efforts, without complaint.

Introduction

Harnessing the force

The number 1,000 or even the word 'Millennium', when associated with a military force has an impressive ring to it. It should be a figure that would impress any man on the street during the dark years of the Second World War and he would surely be happy to know that such a number was associated with our forces rather than with the enemy. The newly-appointed Air Officer Commanding, Sir Arthur Harris had taken the reins of Bomber Command at a time when the odds were stacked against its very existence. Harris was fully aware that he had to impress and impress in a big way if he was going to keep this large resource-consuming giant at the forefront of the fight against Nazi tyranny. Harris had to show that Bomber Command had clout; small, generally ineffective raids up to May 1942 had had little impact in raising civilian morale let alone in the airmen who flew over obscure targets in France, the Low Countries and Germany.

New navigation technology was being introduced as Harris took over, the number of operational bomber squadrons was on the increase and new aircraft such as the Lancaster were beginning to gain a foothold in the inventory. However, if Harris was going to reach that magic number '1,000' he would need aircraft not only from Bomber Command but also from Coastal and Flying

Air Chief Marshal Sir Arthur Harris, the mastermind of the 'Thousand Plan' and saviour of Bomber Command.

The Thousand Bomber Raids

Training Commands. The mainstay of this number would be a stalwart of a bomber, the Vickers Wellington which, even by mid-1942, was still the backbone of Bomber Command and, with the exception of the Whitley and Hampden, was the most prolific bomber in the Operational Training Units as well. On paper, the number was feasible but the variables which would mean success or failure such as weather, serviceability and the skill of enemy defences, to name a few, were all unpredictable factors.

Once established, Harris planned on using his '1,000 Force' for a series of raids during the spring and summer of 1942, but in the end only three were carried out and the first, to Cologne, on May 30/31, was the most successful by some margin. While success was incredibly important, Harris was clearly trying to demonstrate what Bomber Command could do when unleashed *en masse* against a single target and there is little doubt that these 'Thousand Bomber Raids' were a major contribution to the survival and both ultimate success of this powerful force. In fact, Bomber Command never looked back after these large raids and questions about iits effectiveness were not raised at a high level ever again.

Martyn Chorlton

1

Bomber Command

The Lie of the Land in 1942

ormed in July 1936, Bomber Command's early existence relied heavily on a popular slogan of the day; 'the bomber will always get through'. This thinking relied heavily on the fact, (which in part was true at the time) that the average bomber of the mid-1930s had virtually the same performance as the average fighter and as such would receive very little opposition when approaching an enemy target. It was believed that anti-aircraft defences would cause some casualties and that only some of the fighters that had been scrambled in time would harass the bomber on its return journey but, generally, this method of attack was seen as a way of causing total destruction and therefore was the perfect deterrent to future wars.

However, the mid-1930s was a period of rapid military development while the world accelerated into an unavoidable Second World War. Aircraft were part of this technological race which saw both the capacity and the range of bombers increase significantly while fighters gained more horsepower, more effective weapons and improved their general all-round performance to a point where very few bombers could escape on their capability alone.

In July 1936, the RAF was equipped with a range of biplane bombers such as the Hawker Hind, Boulton Paul Overstrand, Fairey Gordon and Hendon, Handley Page Heyford and the Vickers Virginia, the latter having served in various marks since the early 1920s. The eleven Auxiliary squadrons serving with Bomber Command also fielded a collection which included the Hawker Hart and Hind and the Westland Wallace and Wapiti. To think that machines of this calibre would be thrust into a worldwide conflict in just over three years' time must have sent some serious warning signals to the Air Ministry and, as a result, the development of a new breed of bombers had already begun.

The Thousand Bomber Raids

Hawker Hind light bombers of 15 Squadron in 1936 capable of delivering a total bomb load of 510lb. Less than five years later, the squadron was operating the Short Stirling with the capacity to carry 14,000lb of bombs.

By the outbreak of the Second World War in September 1939, the Bomber Command inventory had dramatically changed. The biplane had yielded to the multi-engined monoplane with one exception; the Fairey Battle. The Battle was not the greatest of aircraft and its failings were exposed during the Fall of France in 1940 when losses quickly saw this light bomber despatched to the second line. The remainder, which made up Bomber Command's Order of the Battle in September 1940, were the Bristol Blenheim, Vickers Wellington, Armstrong Whitworth Whitley and Handley Page Hampden. All of these machines were destined to take part in the 'Thousand Bomber' raids, although it was only the reliable and rugged Wellington which would remain in frontline RAF service for the entire war. The Wellington would also be the most prolific type to join the 'Thousand Bomber' raids and it was not until 1943, when production of the four-engined heavies began to gain momentum, that this Barnes Wallis, geodetic-designed classic began to yield.

As well as the aircraft already mentioned, prior to May 1942, four more bombers had joined the Bomber Command inventory. The first, the Short Stirling, entered Bomber Command service in August 1940 followed by another heavy, the Handley Page Halifax, in November. The twin-engined Avro Manchester and first bomber

The Blenheim was the fastest bomber in the RAF inventory at the beginning of the Second World War but by 1942 was already obsolete. However, it would play a key role in the 'Thousand Plan'. These are 57 Squadron machines; by May 1942 the unit had converted to the Vickers Wellington. Bristol Aircraft

variant of the de Havilland Mosquito followed in 1941 while the four-engined Avro Lancaster entered service in early 1942. Further resources, such as the Douglas Boston and Havoc were also available, thanks to 'Lend-Lease' from early 1941. This, on paper, gave Bomber Command a formidable capability which, when harnessed under the right leadership and despatched in an organised fashion, could strike a serious blow against the enemy.

However, while this collection of aircraft appears impressive, Bomber Command still only had one type available in numbers which could deliver a large bomb load even though it was classed as a medium bomber; namely the Wellington. The Blenheim, by 1942, was serving with 2 Group in the light bomber/intruder role, while the Whitley and Hampden, both medium bombers and mainly serving with 4 and 5 Groups respectively lacked the clout, although both were good, respected aircraft

The Thousand Bomber Raids

The Rolls-Royce Vulture-powered Avro Manchester, which thankfully led to the highly successful Lancaster. 99 sorties were flown by this unpopular aircraft during the three 'Thousand Plan' raids.

in their own right. With regard to the new heavy bombers, the Stirling and Halifax were still not available in large numbers; the Manchester proved to be virtually ineffective thanks to mechanical issues and the Lancaster, fresh into service, was still finding its feet, although the latter was already hitting the headlines.

By May 1942, there were five marks of Wellington in operational service; the Bristol Pegasus or Rolls-Royce Merlin-powered Mk IA, which by then was serving with the OTUs (Operational Training Unit); the Mk IC, again serving with OTUs but still on the front line with several squadrons of 1 and 3 Groups; the Merlin-powered Mk II, serving in small numbers with 1 and 4 Groups; the Bristol Hercules-powered Mk III, again in small numbers with two 3 Group squadrons and the Pratt & Whitney Twin Wasp-powered Mk IV, operated by three Polish and two Australian squadrons within 1 Group.

T.R.1335, aka *GEE*

As well as the appointment of a more aggressive AOC and the potential for more modern and capable aircraft at its disposal, Bomber Command was also about to benefit from the introduction of a new navigation aid. Known by the spring of 1942 as *GEE* (aka T.R.1335), this radio navigation system was the brainchild of Dr Robert 'Bob' Dippy, a young scientist who joined the TRE (Telecommunications Research Establishment) in 1936, initially working on radar development at the newly-established RAF Bawdsey Manor, located in plain sight on the Suffolk coast. While the main thrust of Bawdsey was radar development under the charge of James Watt descendent, Robert Alexander Watson-Watt, scientists like Dippy were also looking at other electronic aids such as a potential blind landing system which expanded the experiments at the time that would lead to the highly successful Chain Home Radar network. Dippy's proposed blind landing system would be made up of a pair of transmitting antennas located ten miles apart and positioned on each side of the runway. A master transmitter located directly between them sent a signal to both antennas which made sure that the same signal was broadcast from the outer antennas at exactly the same time. The receiving aircraft would receive the signals which were then displayed via an A-scope

The backbone of Bomber Command, the Vickers Wellington, up to the arrival of the four-engined heavies, was the only aircraft capable of delivering a good sized payload against the enemy. Air Ministry

The Thousand Bomber Raids

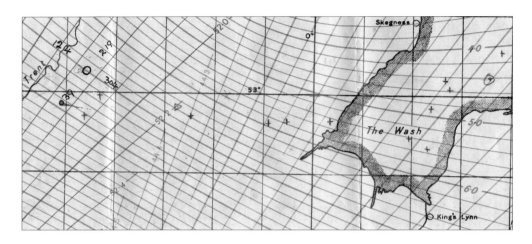

A small sample of an original GEE *Chart used by the navigator of a Lancaster.*
Via Alastair Goodrum

which was an early form of radar display which measured distance from the radar to the target using a horizontal axis. If the aircraft was approaching the centreline of the runway, both signals would be received instantaneously but if the aircraft was off the centreline, one signal would be received before the other and a pair of 'peaks' would appear on the A-scope. Depending on which signal was received first would place the aircraft either closing on the runway or flying away from it.

Supported by Watson-Watt, Dippy put forward his proposal for this new navigational aid to the Air Ministry and subsequently to Bomber Command as early as 1938 but his idea was met with apathy. Bomber Command's response at the time was a little arrogant and somewhat short-sighted. As far as they were concerned, the high standard of training that RAF navigators received at the time, which in part was true, was more than up to the level required, certainly in peacetime. Even as another inevitable world war was on the horizon, there was no thought given to an offensive war and the use of radar was purely aimed at defending rather than attacking which, as we know, would help to save Britain during a certain battle in 1940.

Dippy would continue to improve his navigation aid in 1940, when development was transferred to the TRE outpost at St Aldhelm's Head, south of the village of Worth Matravers, just under five miles west of Swanage on the Dorset coast. In response to early losses suffered by Bomber Command, Dippy was asked to continue his research in an effort to expand his original blind landing system into a long-range position fixing system which could put a bomber much closer to the target than had been achieved to date. On June 24, 1940, Dippy presented his new idea which revolved around a grid system and, as such, it was initially coded 'G' which was expanded to 'GEE' in July 1940 but would still only be referred to as T.R.1335 behind closed doors.

The system was relatively simple; the bomber picked up three signals emitted from a trio of well-spaced ground transmitters. The central transmitter was the master station while the outer two were known as the slaves, these being 'triggered' by pulses from the master. The pulses were then displayed on a cathode ray tube positioned above the navigator's table, complete with an internal measuring device. The difference in time between the signals from the master and each of its slave stations were translated on a special grid which had lines of constant difference. Once this information was collected, the navigator would use his GEE chart, which was covered in hyperbolic lines, to plot the aircraft's position.

Initial testing was promising and the system was showing signs of being accurate up to 300 miles away (as far as the Ruhr from an East Anglian airfield) if the bomber was flying at 10,000ft. Further tests were carried out on October 19, 1940 which just utilised a pair of GEE transmitter systems and even this was accurate up to 110 miles at an altitude of 5,000ft. It was clear that the system had legs and, by the end of 1940, a number of sites across Britain had been requisitioned for GEE ground stations which became officially known as the AMES Type 7000, 30-60 MHz Hyperbolic Navigation System.

Service trials of GEE did not begin until May 15, 1941, the delay partly being due to security, a lack of bombers equipped with it and, more crucially, major problems with making one of the valves needed for the system, the latter not being fully resolved until August. It was that same month when GEE was trialled operationally for the first time when a pair of 115 Squadron Wellingtons were equipped with the device. These two aircraft, along with 27 other Wellingtons, were ordered to attack Mönchengladbach on August 11/12, 1941 and, conveniently, as if to test the

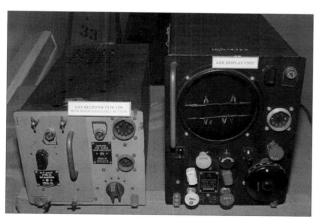

A Type Receiver, T.R.1335 GEE unit on the left and the navigator's cathode ray tube display unit on the right. Via Alastair Goodrum

The Thousand Bomber Raids

GEE system to its maximum, the target was completely cloud-covered. Much improved accuracy was achieved but, during a raid to Hanover the following night, one of the *GEE*-equipped Wellingtons, Z8835 'KO-U' was lost, potentially delivering sensitive equipment on a plate to the enemy. History has told us that this did not happen but the RAF was not prepared to use *GEE* any further until a minimum of 300 bombers could be equipped with the aid. Only days after this final operational trial was carried out, Bomber Command was given the all clear to use *GEE* but mass production would not begin until May 1942. In the meantime though, 300 'hand-made' *GEE* sets would be ready for operational use by January 1, 1942 and these would play their part in the 'Thousand Plan'.

Dr. Robert 'Bob' Dippy, whose general navigation system was developed into the GEE. Purbeck Radar Museum Trust

GEE was not used operationally again until March 8/9, 1942 when 211 bombers attacked Essen with the Krupps Works being the focal point. Unfortunately, a problem which had saved this target from destruction many times before, namely industrial haze, played its part yet again and both the city and works escaped virtually unscathed which was not an encouraging start for the new navigation aid in which the RAF had placed so much faith. Other raids would follow and the first successful *GEE*-led operation took place on the night of March 13/14 when 135 bombers struck Cologne. This raid also saw flares and incendiary bombs dropped accurately on the aiming point which, combined with the effectiveness of *GEE*, was the beginning of a new standard of attack by Bomber Command. The tools and tactics were finally falling into place as Harris prepared to unleash his rapidly improving force in the best way he could.

Defence of the Reich

Night fighter defence

At the beginning of the Second World War, the Luftwaffe was well aware that some form of night air defence would be needed despite the fact that the RAF opened the conflict with a number of audacious daylight raids which it would pay the price for. In late 1939, there was no technology available to the Luftwaffe that could enable them to either intercept or destroy enemy aircraft at

One of the pioneering aircraft of the German night fighter force was the Junkers Jumo-powered Messerschmitt Bf 109D. While never a dedicated night fighter, a number of later marks were active over Germany during May and June 1942.

Oberst Wolfgang Falck (left) the first commander of NJG 1 formed in mid-1940 who was more affectionately known as the father of the Nachtjagdwaffe. He is pictured with night fighter pilot Werner Streib; both of them survived the war.

night but they knew that such a force was needed. As such, the *Dämmerungstaffeln* (Twilight Squadrons) were formed, attached to two wings, namely *Jagdgeschwader* 2 and 26 (JG 2 & 26) and equipped with the Messerschmitt Bf 109D.

Early Bomber Command operations were carried out completely unescorted and up to an infamous raid on Heligoland Bight – when twelve out of a force of 22 Vickers Wellingtons were shot down – were also flown in daylight. It was quite clear that senior pre-war RAF staff had convinced themselves that Bomber Command was an all-conquering force which could easily defend itself against what the Luftwaffe had to offer; this was of course not the case. The only serious option available to Bomber Command was to operate at night which would result in some very inaccurate attacks but the loss rate would significantly reduce as a result. Likewise, in order to combat these night operations, the

Luftwaffe would have to adapt and develop a dedicated night fighter force.

Up to the spring of 1940, the *Dämmerungstaffeln* had only brought down three aircraft and it was clear that this fledgling force was nowhere near effective enough. The Luftwaffe had to raise its game as the threat from attacks on its towns and cities slowly increased. On June 22, 1940, under the command of Oberst Wolfgang Falck of *Zerstörergeschwader76* (ZG 76), *Nachtjagdgeschwader1* (NJG 1) was formed from elements of ZG 1 and ZG 26. NJG I was then expanded into three and deployed with the HQ, Stab./NJG 1 being based at Deelen under Falck's command, I./NJG 1 located at Mönchengladbach under the command of Hptm Günther Radusch, both operating the Messerschmitt Bf 110C and II./NJG 1 under the command of Hptm von Bothmer stationed at Schiphol with the Bf 109D. Just over a week later, NJG 1 was expanding to four groups with II./NJG 1 being redesignated as III./NJG 1 while the former became the extra group at Gütersloh under the command of Hptm Heyse operating the Junkers Ju 88C, a unit which was successfully employed in the long-range intruder operations harassing RAF bombers over England.

The night fighter groups continued to evolve and, despite the fact that the Bf 109

After being brutally relegated from its intended role as a heavy day fighter, the Messerschmitt Bf 110 found itself more suited as a night fighter and through various marks remained in this role until the end of the war.

The Thousand Bomber Raids

While not as prolific as the Bf 110 over Germany in mid-1942 the versatile Junkers Ju 88 would evolve into the mainstay of the night fighter force.

would continue to play a role at night, single-seat fighters were not at home in this environment and, on September 1, 1940, II./NJG 1 was redesignated as I./NJG 2, re-equipped with the more suitable Bf 110 and relocated to Gilze-Rijen from where it would harass the RAF over its own territory. II./NJG 1 was reformed again, this time at Deelen under the command of Hptm Graf von Stillfried und Rattonitz at Deelen, now with the Bf 110. Further expansion took place in October when I./NJG 3 was formed at Vechta under the command of Hptm Radusch, equipped with the Bf 110.

With the Battle of Britain over, the defending night fighter tools were in place and it was a case of honing the skills required to intercept a bomber at night. It would require a high degree of co-operation between ground controllers, flak and searchlight units if it were to be successful. During 1941, this co-operation was paying off and the best tool for the job was a machine that sadly failed in its intended role as a day fighter but proved an ideal machine at night, namely the twin-engined Bf 110. The Ju 88C was also proving to be a formidable aircraft at night, aided by its long range and excellent fire power which caught out many RAF crews over their homeland as well as during night operations over the Continent. By mid-1941, individual Luftwaffe night fighter crews, were already gaining a high number of 'kills' and this 'Defence of the Reich' was fully exploited by the German propaganda machine with many pilots becoming celebrities overnight.

In April 1941, another unit, Stab./NJG 4, was formed at Metz with the Bf 110 under the command of Major Rudolf Stoltenhoff.

The Kammhuber Line

Born in 1896, Josef Kammhuber was a veteran of the First World War, serving with the Bavarian Engineer Battalion and then post-war with the new Reichswehr (Realm Defence 1919-35). By the middle of 1940, Oberst Kammhuber was the commander of a rapidly growing night fighter force and, by October, was in charge of organising a new defensive belt of Germany made up of a number of ground radar units and searchlights. Stage one of Kammhuber's defensive network was a trio of night fighter zones, each supported by two short-range *Würzburg* radar systems. The *Würzburg* gun laying

Josef Kammhuber, the first 'General of the Night Fighters' charged with the defence of the Reich from 1941 to 1943.

radar was introduced into service in 1940 and, in this defensive role, one radar was used to track the position of the night fighter, while a second focussed on the target. The latter also worked closely with local searchlight units to illuminate the target for the night fighter which was a technique simply known as *HelleNachtjagd* (Illuminated Night Fighting) or *HeHaJa*. This technique was then replaced by *Himmelbett* (Four-poster Bed) which differed in the addition of the longer-range *Freya* radar. Compared to the *Würzburg*, which had an effective range of around 20 miles, the powerful *Freya* early-warning radar could reach out up to 120 miles. All of this combined to make a very effective defensive line made up of multiple 'boxes' which became very adept at bringing an experienced night fighter crew within visual range of its prey and, by the middle of 1941, the line stretched from Denmark down to the Swiss border. However, the Kammhuber Line had one major Achilles heel; each 'box' could only deal with one fighter and one enemy aircraft at once. At the time that was not a problem because as the RAF were only sending single aircraft to bomb Germany. It was only a matter of time before the British would find out about this

The short-range Würzburg *radar system which entered service in 1940.*
Bundesarchiv

weakness as there was more intelligence flowing across the Channel than from it and, in early 1942, a Belgian agent kindly delivered a crucial section of map which gave away how the Kammhuber Line was organised. All it would take to breach this defensive line was for Bomber Command to gain a more aggressive commander who would rally his forces and apply them in a more efficient way than had been achieved up to this point.

Kammhuber continued to expand and improve his defensive line but his efforts

An example of the Würzburg-Riese *(Giant Würzburg) radar system which was introduced in late 1941.*

were not matched with an increase in night fighter units. Germany was fighting a war on multiple fronts and the need for such units in the Eastern Front and the Mediterranean meant that the situation could only be improved through efficiency rather than an increase in weaponry. As such, the Kammhuber Line began to become even more sophisticated when the more powerful *Würzburg-Riese* (Giant *Würzburg*) was introduced in late 1941. The *Würzburg-Riese* had a range of 50 miles which allowed each defensive zone to extend to a depth of 60 miles and they were deployed in front of and behind the zone in company with the *Freya*.

By May 1942, the Kammhuber Line consisted of a *Freya* front line which stretched along the Belgian, Dutch and North German coast assisted by 150cm and 200cm searchlight regiments and backed up with an array of multi-calibre anti-aircraft guns. It was the task of this first line of defence to report on the number, altitude and direction of the bombers and, in response, the appropriate night fighter units would be scrambled to engage them in the main illuminated searchlight belt. All areas in between the front line and the searchlight belt and beyond were designated as dark fighting areas called *DunkleNachtjagd* or *DuNaJa* (Dark Night Fighting).

Another night fighting method developed during 1941 was called *Konaja* (*KombinierteNachtjagd* (Combined Night Fighting)). One of the few places the RAF expected to be attacked by an enemy fighter was during the final bombing run, when flak was more likely to be at its fiercest. Naturally, this was not an environment that a night fighter wanted to enter and its crew would be more than happy for the flak to do its work rather than run the gauntlet of being shot down themselves. A new system was introduced using observation posts (*Flukos*) which would make an initial contact with the approaching bomber. Once the bomber reached a certain point, the night fighter was scrambled and given orders to orbit until Falk rangefinders established the enemy's height and direction using a *Seeburg* glass plotting map. The latter was a labour intensive affair which plotted the information

Female personnel in a Würzburg *control centre with their light projectors in front of them which projected onto a glass map table* Seeburg. Bundesarchiv

received from the *Würzburgs*, one of which was tracking the enemy bomber, while the other followed the night fighter. The positions of the two aircraft were projected onto the Seeburg map with light projectors positioned by the controller through information received from the *Würzburg* through headphones. A ground controller would then talk the night fighter to the target and, as it closed, the pilot would order the flak guns to stop firing within a certain sector. With the assistance of searchlights, the night fighter would then make its attack but, in practice, very few attacks were successful because of the delay between the pilot's instruction being given and received by the gunners below. *Konaja* zones were active around Bremen, Cologne and the Ruhr, Kiel, Hamburg, Frankfurt, Mannheim and Berlin; the latter had its own *HeNaJa* searchlight belt to protect its western flank.

On May 5, 1942, Hitler issued an executive order to redeploy large numbers of searchlights from the Kammhuber Line to towns and cities across Germany which had been suffering under Harris' new, concentrated bombing methods. The Kammhuber Line would stand until the end of the war and was certainly virtually intact for the raid on Cologne. Its construction was incredibly expensive and it was equally costly to operate, not to mention the cost of the thousands of personnel needed to support it. If it had been invested in properly from the outset, the RAF, even with the introduction of the bomber 'stream', would have suffered much greater losses at the hands of larger numbers of night fighters. For example in the

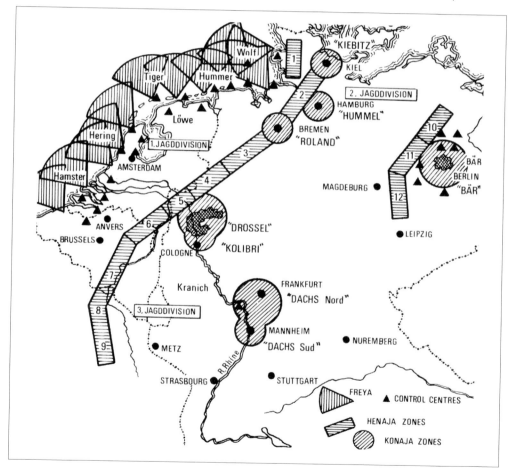

The Kammhuber Line in 1942. Ian Allan Ltd

summer of 1941, the total night fighter strength defending the Reich was 265 aircraft, of which only approximately half were serviceable. Hitler was constantly re-positioning his assets which continued to weaken the defence of Germany but, as defeat approached, ironically, these forces could be concentrated and the night fighter threat only ever increased for the RAF aircrews right up to the end of the Second World War.

The only segments of the Kammhuber Line system that were missing were a reliable IFF (Identification Friend or Foe) system and the ability for the night fighter to carry its own radar. This was solved by a new airborne radar named *Lichtenstein* SN-2. This system had already been successfully trialled when Oblt Ludwig Becker of 4./NJG 1 shot down a 301 Squadron Wellington near NieuweSchans on August 8/9, 1941, with a *Lichtenstein*-equipped Dornier Do 215B. The system would not be fully operational until early 1942, by which time, Bomber Command was attempting to change from what was considered an ineffective to a highly effective arm of the British war machine.

3

'The Thousand Plan'

The final countdown

Harris' movements and meetings leading up to the now named Operation *Millennium* were well-documented, beginning with an invitation from Winston Churchill on May 17 to dine with him at Chequers. It was after this dinner that Harris presented the PM with his thousand bomber plan. Churchill was very enthusiastic about the idea, to the point where he was more than willing to accept losses of up to 100 bombers which took even Harris aback as he only expected a maximum of 60 aircraft to be lost.

The following day, bolstered by the fact that he had Churchill's full support, Harris approached the Chief of the Air Staff, Air Chief Marshal Sir Charles Portal, with the plan. Knowing full well how many aircraft he had available, Harris was under no illusion that, to make this raid work, he would have to rely on Coastal Command for a contribution. Harris asked Portal to confirm with Churchill that the Admiralty would not be obstructive with regard to such a request. On May 19, Portal, who had already discussed the position with Churchill, received the following message from the PM; 'I mentioned the Thousand Plan to the First Sea Lord*, last night. I am sure that he will not be any obstacle to the use of Coastal Command, unless there is something special on.' Portal quickly passed the contents of the message on to Harris who immediately set to work planning the biggest operation of both his career and the RAF's history.

On May 20, Harris penned the following to all relevant Group, Coastal Command, Flying Training Command and Army Co-Operation Command AOCs; 'It is proposed at about the full moon to put over the maximum possible force of bombers on a single and extremely important town in Germany with a view to wiping it out in one

---

*Sir Dudley Pound

The Thousand Bomber Raids

night, or at the most two. The idea of the operation is to saturate the ARP arrangements at the objective as to cause a complete and uncontrollable conflagration throughout the target area. To what end the maximum number of incendiary bombs would comprise the load, HE being used only when essential as a make-weight towards an economical load'. Harris also stated that the date of the attack would be on May 28 or the most suitable following night and ordered that no leave was to be granted until Operation *Millennium* was over. In the same message, Harris set about the all-important task of gathering the numbers of aircraft that each group had available; all would be revealed the following day.

Air Marshal Sir William Welsh, the AOC of Flying Training Command, was the first to respond, on May 21. It was a conservative offer, although Flying Training Command was not exactly awash with bombers and the ones that they had were old and tired. Welsh only thought he could provide up to eight Wellington IAs, nine Whitley I and IIIs (these machines were barely able to perform training duties let alone a full-scale operation) and at least 13 Hampdens. It was small beer but every little helped and Welsh backed his offer up with a number of fully trained navigators.

The same day, a more substantial offer was received from Air Marshal Sir Philip Benner Joubert de la Ferté, the AOC of Coastal Command. Joubert de la Ferté wrote to Harris stating that he could provide 250 aircraft, comprising a pair of Wellington and Whitley squadrons (which were already detached to Bomber Command), a quartet of Hampden squadrons, two Beaufort squadrons plus a number of Hudsons and OTU machines.

Next to respond were the AOCs of 91 and 92 Group (both formed on May 11, 1942) both of which controlled a number of Bomber Command OTUs and from where Harris was expecting a substantial number of aircraft. Neither disappointed, 91 Group (under the command of Air Commodore H S P Walmsley) offered 200 aircraft while 92 Group (Air Commodore H A Haines) promised a further 130; all of them Wellingtons.

With his main group numbers easily at hand, Harris could now beginning totalling up how many aircraft he potentially had at his disposal. They were as follows; 1 Group (100), 3 Group (160), 4 Group (130), 5 Group (95), 91 Group (200), 92 Group (130), Coastal Command (250) and Flying Training Command (21) which made a grand total of 1,086 aircraft. This number must have come as a great relief to Harris who had yet to include 2 Group and Army Co-Operation Command's contribution of its Blenheims, not to mention additional support from Fighter Command.

Target Hamburg and Operation *Banquet*

On May 23, news of the impending thousand bomber raid became known to a

A typical training aircraft belonging to 12 OTU at Chipping Warden, one of many which took part in 'Thousand Plan'. This Wellington III, Z1732 'FQ-S' was delivered to the unit in April 1942 and was SOC until May 1947; a rare survivor.

much wider audience when Operation Order No.147, signed by the Deputy AOC Bomber Command, Air Marshal Sir Robert Saundby, was released from HQ Bomber Command at High Wycombe. Hamburg would be the primary target; however, the secondary target would be Cologne should poor weather be reported over the primary.

Keeping the size of operation secret right up to take-off was now the challenge with so many aircraft, units and personnel involved. Obviously, a large number of units, especially the OTUs, would have to relocate to airfields in more easterly positions from where they would operate alongside the resident squadron and be controlled by the relevant group.

To keep security leaks to a minimum, the RAF decided to carry out Operation *Banquet* as a large training exercise. *Banquet* would be an ideal 'umbrella' to cover the movements of large numbers of OTU Wellingtons and any re-organisations within individual groups.

With aircraft kept firmly on the ground because of poor weather, May 24 was not a day to be wasted as group and squadron commanders read Order No.147 in detail. Initially, there was more attention paid to how and where a large number of bombers were going to locate beginning with Coastal Command who prepared to deploy over 100 aircraft to Bomber Command airfields. Army Co-Operation Command would move eight Blenheims from 13 Squadron to operate with 18 Squadron at Wattisham and a further eight from 614 (County of Glamorgan) Squadron to operate with 114 Squadron also stationed at Wattisham. The aircraft contributed from Flying Training Command would see their Wellingtons move to Feltwell (3 Group), the Whitleys to Driffield (4 Group) and the Hampdens to Syerston (5 Group).

The deployment of the OTU resources would be far more complicated, beginning with 91 Group which would move the following; 18 OTU from Bramcote to Hemswell, 21 OTU from Moreton-in-the-Marsh to Snaith and 22 OTU from Wellesbourne Mountford to Elsham Wolds (all 1 Group airfields) and 23 OTU from Pershore to Stradishall, Oakington and Bourn (all 3 Group).

The Admiralty pulls the plug!

Confidence in the fact that Harris' vision of a hammer blow against the Third Reich

One of the more 'exotic' contributions to Operation Millennium were the Douglas Havocs of 23 Squadron 11 Group, which carried out intruder operations against a number of German night fighter airfields.

was rapidly coming together took a major blow of its own on May 25. Completely unexpectedly and against the tide of optimism which had been received on May 19, came the news that The Admiralty had declined the use of Coastal Command aircraft for the operation. This would have come as a major shock to all of the Bomber Command planners but, undeterred, Harris immediately set about re-organising his remaining forces in an attempt to make up a shortfall of 250 aircraft. Although it was less of an impact, Flying Training Command also delivered the news on that day that they could only provide a total of 14 bombers made up of seven Hampdens, four Wellington and three Whitleys.

A rapid revision of the numbers of aircraft available resulted in the following; 1 Group (110), 3 Group (160), 4 Group (157), 5 Group (105), 91 Group (250), 92 Group (120) and Flying Training Command (14). This made a total of 916; not enough if Harris was going to deliver. To make up the shortfall, conversion and training flights, along with student crews from the OTUs, would have to be included.

The day was destined to finish on a more upbeat note following a meeting about intruder operations where 2 Group confirmed their commitment by offering 30 Blenheims while 11 Group promised 25 Bostons/Havocs and a dozen long-range Hurricane IICs.

The final order

As the window of opportunity with regard to the full moon period approached, Operation Order No.148 was issued on May 26. Now revised, thanks to The Admiralty, the order was a comprehensive one, broken down into 34 sections. The order is summarised as follows; Information (Part 1 to 3) – the target will be HAMBURG (described as an attack of 'exceptional weight') and Part 3 stated 'An attack in such force has never remotely been approached in past either by ourselves or by the enemy. It should strike a severe blow to the morale of the German people in addition to causing unprecedented damage to the most important single industrial city in Germany.' Intention (Part 4) – 'To destroy the port and city of HAMBURG.'; Execution (Part 5 to 8) – Code Name, 'This operation will be known as the THOUSAND PLAN.', Date 'The Operation will take place on the night of May 27/28 or on the first suitable night thereafter until the night of May 31/June 1, 1942.', Alternative Target 'If conditions are unfavourable for an attack on HAMBURG, COLOGNE will be attacked. The decision as to which target is to be attacked will be communicated to all concerned no later than 1200hrs on the day of the operation.'; Attack on Cologne (Part 9 to 16) – Route to and from Target, 'All aircraft will be routed as follows (Part 17):- BASE – OUDURP (51°47'N, 03°50'E) – TARGET – EUSKIRCHEN (50°38'N, 06°47'E) – NOORDLAND (51°38'N, 03°36'E) – BASE,

Compared to other bomber-type aircraft, the interior of the Short Stirling was vast. This is the view aft towards the mid-upper turret.

Timing 'ZERO HOUR will be the time that the attack on the target begins. The attack is to end at Z plus 1 hour 30 minutes. ZERO HOUR in Double summer Time will be notified to all concerned as early as possible on the day of the operation and not later than 1700hrs.', 'Nos.1 and 3 Groups are to open the attack with all available T.R. aircraft at Z hours. The attack is to be completed by Z hours plus 15 minutes.', 'All available heavies from Nos 4 and 5 Groups are to attack at Z hours plus 1 hour 15 minutes. This attack is to be completed by Z hours plus 1 hour 30 minutes.' Rules for Turning Back 'In order to avoid aircraft which are late owing to delays in taking off, or through faulty navigation or any other reason, being intercepted in daylight during the return journey, the following rule is to be observed: All aircraft are to turn for home not later than Z plus 1 hour 45 minutes, wherever they may be and whether they have dropped their bombs or not.', Aiming Points (See supplied map) 1 and 3 Groups to bomb 'A', 4 and 92 Group to bomb 'X' and 5 and 91 Group to bomb 'Y', 'If crews are unable to identify COLOGNE they are to set course direct for ESSEN where the aiming point is STOAT 'B' with any built up area seen in the RUHR as a last resort target. Route home for aircraft attacking ESSEN or last resort targets is not to be the route home given in Part 17, but is to be direct, avoiding, as far as possible, heavily defended zones' (This section was amended on May 29 to include COLOGNE as the new primary target). Height of Attack 'At discretion of AOCs but the minimum height is to be 8,000ft'. Bomb Loads 'All aircraft are to carry the maximum economical load of 4lb and 30lb incendiary bombs, made up as necessary with HE bombs. Where HE bombs must be used to make loads, large HC and GP bombs are to be given preference and in any event, none smaller than the 500lb should be carried. All incendiaries are to be dropped in stick with distributor setting of 0.1 seconds', the following was added on May 29, 'As many as possible incendiaries x4lb are to be dropped by aircraft of 3, 4 and 5 Groups and the greater proportion is to be carried by aircraft in the first wave.'

Leading up to this raid, Britain was operating under Double Summer Time (two hours ahead of GMT); a system that was introduced from the summer of 1941. Harris was particularly concerned about the amount of pure darkness he had to operate in, which was reduced by 45 minutes after sunset and prior to sunrise as the twilight period took hold. It was imperative that the bomber force was over enemy territory in darkness otherwise they would have to contend with day and night fighters, the former being an unnecessary risk. In theory, the entire force would have a six hour-long darkness period to operate in but if all units followed their individually briefed schedules to the letter, the whole operation should be completed within five hours.

The route to and from the target was designed to be as simple as possible combined with spending the shortest amount of time as possible over enemy territory. The start point would be Southwold on the Suffolk coast followed by a straight-in approach of approximately 245 miles. Once the aircraft had bombed, the aircraft would make a 90° turn to starboard which was maintained for approximately 17 miles before another final 90° turn to starboard and a then direct route home to Orfordness, again located on the Suffolk coast. The 17-mile space was designed into the plan so as to avoid the chances of an aerial collision. The route was not without its dangers and eleven night fighter airfields were positioned on the route, these being; Bonn-Hangelar, Deelen, Eindhoven, Gilze-Rijen, Juvincourt, Schiphol, Soesterburg, St Trond, Twente, Vechta and Venlo. A leading intruder force would be allocated to all of these airfields as targets prior and during the early stages of operation. The task was allocated to 2 Group and Fighter Command who would carry out their own separate and combined operations.

Another significant feature of this raid was time over the target window which was a mere 90 minutes. The idea was that this amount of bombers presented to the enemy defences in such concentration would overload them and in theory reduce the number of targets exposed to the air and ground defences. It was common knowledge by this point that the *Würzburg* sectors could only handle one bomber at a time and if that sector could be flooded by bombers then the odds of being attacked was reduced by some margin. On the down side, the risk of an aerial collision between bombers was increased but on the advice of a number of 'boffins', this was deemed an acceptable risk and you had considerably more chance of being shot down by an enemy fighter rather than being brought down by another bomber.

Understandably, those aircraft operating with *GEE* installed were given different instructions on how to carry out the actual raid. Wellingtons and Stirlings of 3 Group would be *GEE* equipped and all responsibility for planting their incendiaries in the Neumarkt in Cologne was down to them and the ultimate accuracy of the raid. 3 Group had orders and I quote 'bombs will be released visually on the homing run when the target is identified and positioned confirmed by T.R. 1335...' In contrast, the non-*GEE* machines of 92 Group such as 14, 16, 25 and 26 OTUs were simply instructed to bomb between Zero Hour plus one hour and 15 minutes. In contrast, 4 Group's instructions were more precise and with only a couple of exceptions, each unit taking part was only given a ten-minute bombing window from an altitude that only varied by 500ft. The seasoned 1 and 5 Groups' approach to this operation was of equal accuracy. Under normal operational conditions, the differences between each group's approach would be clear for all to see during the post raid analysis but, for this operation, it was not about individual success but rather that effect of the entire raid on the target.

Banquet continues

The first indication that 'something was up' was the arrival from Elgin, on May 26, of 14 Wellingtons of 20 OTU at Stanton Harcourt located six miles west of Oxford. The distance these machines had to travel led to the unit being ordered to its advanced operating base a day early while the rest of the OTUs were instructed to move to their allocated stations on May 27. Not all Bomber Command OTUs would take part in the raid. For example 13, 17, 19 and 24 OTUs would not be taking part while 29 OTU at North Luffenham, which had only formed on April 21, was insufficiently established to take part.

Operation *Banquet* was effectively a 'last-ditch' effort to throw every serviceable aircraft against an impending German invasion and, as such, was brought into effect after the Fall of France in July 1940. The operation would literally call up every operational and second line aircraft that could fly and in the latter's case, could be made to drop bombs. Everything from a heavy bomber to an Elementary Flying Training School Tiger Moth could be called to arms and it was under this shroud that

Handley Page Hampdens of 14 OTU are scattered as far as the eye can see at RAF Cottesmore. 14 OTU contributed to all three operations in healthy numbers.

the mass movement of OTU bombers was carried out on May 27. This movement of OTU machines would be the largest 'exercise' and most significant under the guise of Operation *Banquet* but, luckily for Britain, was never used in anger.

While this 'rehearsal' of Operation *Banquet* was a success, a large number of OTU machines still operated from their parent airfields and some did not relocate at all, such as 27 OTU at Lichfield whose 21 Wellingtons all operated from the Staffordshire airfield despite being one of the farthest west to take part in the raid.

The vast majority of OTU crews were under no illusion that this was not just an exercise and orders stated that they should fly fully equipped along with the arrival of large numbers of bombs and incendiaries at their respective stations clearly indicated that this was going to be a proper 'live' operation for them. The mass migration of OTU aircraft generally went well from a flying point of view and only one Flying Training Command Hampden crashed *en route* to Syerston. It was only after they had arrived that problems began to surface with regard to the crews' own flying equipment and in some cases there was a distinct lack of operational equipment fitted to their aircraft. Problems were overcome although a number of aircraft, mainly those provided by Flying Training Command, were found to be unsuitable to take part, these included Hampdens at Syerston and a batch of tired Whitleys.

Unbeknown to all crews of Bomber Command, HQ were planning the operation to begin on the evening of May 27 but the weather was against it and, at 1030hrs, the plug was pulled. It was the same story on May 28 as the weather continued its poor spell.

Taking stock

While the weather continued to be ultimately in charge of when this great operation would be launched, Bomber Command took stock of the forces at its disposal on May 29. In group order, 1 Group had eight squadrons, 2 Group eight squadrons, 3 Group 14 Squadrons, 4 Group seven squadrons, 5 Group ten squadrons and finally the original 8 Group with one squadron. On paper at least, Bomber Command could draw 597 aircraft from these squadrons but would still be relying heavily on making up the magic 1,000 with the aid of the training groups. On top of that, it issued the call to conversion units and various flights and men who had not flown for months found themselves being removed from their desks with orders to draw flying kit in an effort to make up even more crews.

It was another difficult decision day regarding the weather as there was an obvious sign of improvement over France and, closer to home while Hamburg and Cologne looked doubtful. At 1305hrs, the signal declaring that operations were off for tonight, was sent from High Wycombe. The pressure was mounting on Harris to maintain the bomber offensive as there had not been a full-scale raid since Mannheim on May 19/20. Harris now had multiple concerns; he was well aware that if he did not despatch a raid of some kind soon the Germans would suspect that something major was about occur and, in theory, jeopardise the operation. On the other hand, he was fully aware of how precious each of his crews and aircraft were to the success of the operation and Bomber Command could ill afford to lose one more machine if one thousand was going to be achieved. Harris promised himself earlier that he would not despatch any crews the night before the 'big' operation but, on the night of May 29/30 he felt had no choice other than to sanction a 77-strong raid against the Gnome & Rhone factory in Paris. A further 72 aircraft were also despatched on minor operations to Cherbourg, Dieppe, minelaying off Copenhagen and the Frisians and a trio of 'Nickels' over France. Four Wellingtons, two Stirlings and one Halifax were lost; out of these seven aircraft, only three survived to become POWs while 41 men perished including the commanding officer of 156 Squadron, Wg Cdr F G R Heath. These crews had paid the price for secrecy; the 'Thousand Plan' was still on and the weather was about to turn.

The most important 'Met' brief

It was at 0920hrs on Saturday May 30, 1942 that Harris sat down in the Operations Room at High Wycombe to receive the first of three weather reports for the day from Group Captain M Spence, the Chief Bomber Command Meteorologist. Summarising, Spence's report declared that Germany had a great deal of thundery cloud in the north west which thinned towards the centre of Rhine; France was generally covered in convection cloud which would disperse during the night while the 'Home Base' would also experience convection cloud and local thundery showers.

The forecast was encouraging and there was every chance that it could change for better as the day progressed. Harris lit a cigarette, walked over to the large operations map on the wall and traced his finger across it until it stopped at Cologne. Turning to his Senior Air Staff Officer, Air Vice Marshal R Saundby, Harris said that the 'Thousand Plan' would be on for tonight. Very aware that even though he had made this decision, the weather was far from ideal, he later wrote the following, 'It was by no means the greatest risk that a commander in the field had had to take in war but it was a considerable risk.'

Despite his decision being made early that morning, it was not until midday that the 'warning order' was issued to all group commanders complete with Zero Hour time of 0055hrs. A controller at HQ issued this information through a secure phone link to all of the receiving group controllers simultaneously which was then backed up teleprinter. By this time, it was already time for Harris to sit down and listen to Spence's second 'Met' report of the day at 1300hrs. As if to support Harris' decision to select Cologne as the target, Spence stated that Cologne was presently covered in 7/10ths cloud but was likely to clear while Hamburg hid beneath an immovable 8/10ths cloud. Spence also suggested that there was a chance that half of 1 Group's airfields, located in north Lincolnshire, would be covered in fog. The latter was least of Harris's concerns.

Every Bomber Command station with a unit taking part in the 'Thousand Plan' was now a hive of activity as station commanders held conferences. All crews were informed that the operation was on and groundcrews worked even harder to get as many machines as possible serviceable. The latter would not be fully confirmed until every aircraft was flown during the mid-afternoon on a night-flying test to make sure everything was working as it should and, if not, the fault was reported and rectified as quickly as possible.

At 1700hrs, Harris received his final weather report of the day; it was the best of the day so far, reporting that there would be broken cloud over Cologne which, by nightfall, would feature large breaks. Thunderstorms and a large amount of cloud were reported for the trip to the target while the situation should have improved further on the way home. Harris, with regard to the weather, was the happiest he had been all day and felt confident that he had made the right decision.

Pre-match tally

Squadrons across Bomber Command were being briefed and, after days of speculation, the target was revealed (much to the relief of many), while at HQ a final prediction of the amount of aircraft that would actually take part was made. 1 Group, which included the OTU machines of 91 Group, had 150 aircraft; 2 Group which included Army Co-Operation Command had 50 aircraft; 3 Group which included the OTU aircraft of 91 and 92 Group presented 235 aircraft; 4 Group 155, 5 Group 157, 91 Group 261 and 92 Group 94 aircraft making a grand total of 1,102 bombers. Considering the total was only 916 on May 25, this figure was impressive and is a reflection of the hard graft that the groundcrews had put in to help make the 'Thousand Plan' a success.

Final briefings

Meanwhile, the briefings continued across the country, beginning with the big reveal by the station commander, who was followed by the squadron navigation officers.

A typical 128cm FlaK 49 anti-aircraft gun capable of firing a round up to 35,000ft, at a rate of eight to ten rounds per minute. Tiergarten, Berlin 1945.

It was the latter who delivered the details of the operations such as flak and searchlight locations, potential areas where balloons were used and, for those relevantly equipped, *GEE* charts. The route to the forming up point, which was just prior to crossing the coast at Southwold, was also presented, along with all the necessary timings working back from the official Z Hour time of 0055hrs.

The 'Met' man would follow and then an intelligence officer would deliver all of the known information about the German defences. By this time, the Kammhuber line was fully understood, as was *Freya*, and following the successful Bruneval Raid (Operation *Biting*) on February 27/28, 1942 a lot more was known about the *Würzburg* radar system as well. Great emphasis would have been made to the crews of all the benefits of remaining tightly in a bomber stream as the defending night fighters were radar controlled and, as such, would potentially only be successfully guided towards lone targets.

Cologne was a seasoned target with regard to its own defences and a great deal of information was already known to the RAF. The city had at least 450 flak guns ranging from light 20mm, to medium 37mm and the standard heavy guns beginning with the efficient 88mm and the 105 and the 128mm. The latter was capable of sending a round up to 35,000ft at a rate of eight to ten rounds per minute. All of these guns worked in co-operation with a number of 150cm and 200cm searchlights.

The information known about night fighter units, their strength and their locations was reasonably up to date but could never be 100% accurate. However, post-war historians have presented the following beginning with NJG 1, stationed at Deelen, St Trond, Stade, Twente and Venlo which had approximately 49 serviceable Bf 110s available and a potential further 16 Bf 110s allocated to reserve training. NJG 2, located at Leeuwarden and Ardorf had a total of 21 operational night fighters while NJG 3 at Stade, Schleswig/Jagel and Luneburg could boast 59 serviceable Bf 110s. Finally NJG 4 which had serviceable Bf 110s to its name but at the time of this operation was in training. Regardless of the accuracy of the information presented to the crews at the time, the majority of them were already familiar with what the Luftwaffe had to offer them and were under no illusion that this would not be an easy trip despite the reassurances of the large bomber stream.

One thing that all of the briefings had in common that evening was a message from Harris, most likely read out by the station commander as follows:

'The Force of which you are about to take part tonight is at least twice the size and more than four times the carrying capacity of the largest air force ever before concentrated on one objective. You have the opportunity therefore to strike a blow at the enemy which will resound, not only throughout Germany, but throughout the world. In your hands be the means of destroying a major part of the resources by which the enemy's war effort is maintained. It depends, however, upon each individual crew whether full concentration is achieved.

Press home your attack to your precise objectives with the utmost determination and resolution in the full knowledge that, if you individually succeed, the most shattering and devastating blow will have been delivered against the very vitals of the enemy.

Let him have it, right on the chin.'

4

The Raid – Operation *Millennium*

Cologne (May 30/31)

Release the intruders

The honour of being the first aircraft to take off for the largest bombing raid in history befell a pilot of 114 Squadron; Plt Off Strasser in Blenheim IV, V5635. Strasser and his crew, Plt Off Allen and Sgt Harrison, lifted from West Raynham's runway at 2121hrs tasked for an attack on the night fighter airfield at Vechta, 14 miles east of Essen. Vechta had been the home of 1 Gruppe, Nachtjagdgeschwader 3 (1./NJG3) since October 1940 and, by May 1942, were operating the Bf 110 and Dornier Do 217 under the command of Hptm Hans-Dietrich Knoetzsch. Vechta was in a strategically important location in central Germany and this airfield, along with several others this evening, would be the main focus of 2 Group's Blenheims; the main objective being to divert night fighter attention away from the heavy bombers. Of the 18 aircraft tasked from 114 Squadron, eight would attack Vechta, eight Bonn-Hangelar and two Twente. One of the busiest airfields in Germany during the Second World War, Bonn-Hangelar, was located 15 miles south of Cologne, while Twente, located four miles north of Enschede, Netherlands was the home of III./NJG 1, equipped with the Bf 110 and Do 215.

A combination of fog and low cloud ensured that only one Blenheim of the eight aircraft detailed to attack Vechta found the night fighter airfield. Sqn Ldr Gauthier in Z7761 'O' attacked from 3,000ft, the bombs being seen '.....to score hits near a row of lights'. To add insult, one aircraft failed to return from the Vechta raid; V5645 'R' crewed by Plt Off J J Fox RNZAF and Sgts J Leonard and A Smithson. Although

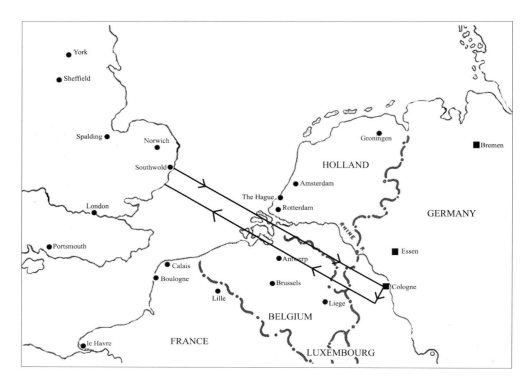

Regardless of their location in England all three waves of bombers, which took part in Operation Millennium*, should have followed this straightforward route from the Suffolk coast direct to Cologne and back again.*

Fox is believed to have survived the initial crash, he was laid to rest alongside his crew in the Sage War Cemetery. Sgt Mallett and crew in Z6161 'Z' were also unable to locate Vechta but instead attacked Ardorf (Wittmund) from 1,000ft; they believed that their bombs had fallen on the runways.

In contrast, the eight Blenheims tasked with attacking Bonn-Hangelar achieved considerably more success. Sqn Ldr Iredale in Z7356 'F' attacked from 2,000ft at 0039hrs and scored hits on buildings on the eastern side of airfield while Flt Lt Molesworth in V5155 'J' planted a long stick across the field. Flt Sgt Shackleton at the controls of Z7319 'P' attacked from 3,000ft and bombs were seen to explode in a line across the centre of the airfield while Sgt Glen in V6431 'M' achieved the same, although at least one bomb exploded amongst some buildings. Sgt Dawes V6264 'X' also hit Bonn-Hangelar from 3,000ft, the bombs were believed to have fallen in the vicinity of the runways and, on the way home, the Wop/AG, Sgt Green,

A typical Bristol Blenheim IV of 114 Squadron pictured at West Raynham a few days before Operation Millennium. *Via the late Graham Warner*

machine-gunned a pair of search lights at Cologne, extinguishing one of them. The only exception was Wg Cdr Pollard and crew in V6262 'G' who bombed a bridge in Bonn, 3 miles southwest of the airfield, from 1,800ft at 0120hrs. The Wop/AG, Sgt Townsend saw burst on the bridge and a few on an island in the river.

The final two 114 Squadron Blenheims attacked Twente; the first, L8800 'C' flown by Sgt Causley, attacked from 3,000ft at 0045hrs; bombs were seen to burst across the airfield. Sgt J L Mitchell and crew in V6337'D' followed at 2,000ft at 0103hrs; their bombs were observed to burst amongst a number buildings.

It was not the greatest of successes for 114 Squadron but the AOC 2 Group was happy because, during the day of May 31, the following signal was received, 'Preliminary investigations reveal that E/A activity on aerodromes attacked by Blenheims on Saturday night was far below normal – there should be no doubt that

Early victims:- Plt Off R M Cundy (left) with his crew, Sgt Stevenson and Sgt Bennet who failed to return from a raid to Juvincourt in Blenheim IV, N3616 'R'. Via the late Graham Warner

your share in 'Intruder' activities was most appreciated – congratulations to all crews participating.'

614 Squadron operating from West Raynham were the next machines from 2 Group to take to the air, led by Sqn Ldr B R MacNamara and crew in Blenheim IV, Z5882 'L' at 2130hrs. MacNamara left first because he had been detailed to join 114 Squadron in their attack on Vechta but, like his colleagues, he also failed to locate the target because of very bad weather and poor visibility and was forced to drop his bombs on Norderney Island.

The remaining seven 614 Squadron Blenheims tasked this night were given Twente as their target and all but two found the airfield. Only Wg Cdr R E S Skelton

Ofw Heinz Strüning of E./NJG 2 who was responsible for bringing down Plt Off R D Pegram's 23 Squadron Boston III during a raid on Deelen airfield.

and crew in N3536 'A' failed to locate the target and brought their bombs back to West Raynham. The five who did manage to attack Twente were ably assisted by the flare path being lit as a number of enemy fighters were in the circuit being signalled by a ground controller.

The next of the 2 Group departures was 18 Squadron at Wattisham who, along with the crews of 13 Squadron, were briefed by the Station Commander, Gp Capt F J Mellergh AFC at 1730hrs. Both units' targets were the night fighter airfields at Juvincourt, St Trond and Venlo. Juvincourt, located 15 miles northwest of Reims, was known to being used as a forward operating base for night fighters but at this time no permanent unit was in place. St Trond (aka Saint-Trond-Brustern, Brustern or Sint-Truiden) was a major night fighter airfield located 20 miles northwest of Liege and was the home of II./NJG1 which operated the Bf 110. Located three miles due east of its namesake, on the Dutch/German border, Venlo was home of I./NJG1 which also operated the Bf 110. It was vital that operations from these three airfields were disrupted as much as possible.

Wattisham's contribution to this raid began at 2219hrs when Flt Lt F M Thorne and crew in Blenheim IV, V7304 'T' took off, bound for Juvincourt. Five aircraft were allocated this target, four of which located and bombed the airfield. Flt Lt A K McCurdy and crew in V6317 'G' bombed at just 300ft just as an enemy aircraft was landing and, as a result, claimed the machine as destroyed. Eight more aircraft were despatched to St Trond including future VC winner, Sqn Ldr H G Malcolm and crew in Z7351 'A'. All with the exception of V5683 'D', which returned early with R/T failure and Z7279 'H', which bombed a lit airfield near Brussels, hit their targets and returned home safely. Finally, the remaining six 614 Squadron Blenheims all successfully found and bombed Venlo airfield with a bomb load comprising a pair of 250lb, eight x 40lb and 24 x 9lb bombs in perfect weather conditions.

A Wellington IC of 103 Squadron based at Elsham Wolds in north Lincolnshire. The squadron contributed 19 bombers to Operation Millennium *and almost all returned safely. One aircraft was lost and another, which diverted to Kirmington, crashed the following day with loss of four crew.* A G Hart via Tom Allett

The Thousand Bomber Raids

At 2230hrs, the first of seven 13 Squadron Blenheims, flown by Fg Off Rothwell and crew in N3545 'K' took off from Wattisham. Four Blenheims were tasked to attack Juvincourt, two against St Trond and a single machine to Venlo. Three out of four successfully bombed Juvincourt but unfortunately Plt Off R M Cundy and crew in N3616 'R' failed to return. It is believed that the bomber crashed off the French coast *en route* as two of the crew, Cundy and Sgt Stevenson, are buried in Boulogne and Calais respectively. The body of the air gunner, Sgt Bennet, was never found, and so he is remembered on the Runnymede Memorial. The remaining three Blenheims all found their targets, bombed accordingly and returned safely to Wattisham.

Also worthy of mention were the Hawker Hurricane IICs of 1 and 3 Squadrons, both under 11 Group operating out of Manston. While 3 Squadron's contribution to the operation's night intruder forays are sketchy, 1 Squadron did carry out patrol over Arras, Berck, Béthune, Le Cretoy, Lille, Lens, St Trond and Vilno. W/O G Scott claimed to have damaged a Ju 88 at St Trond, eight trains were claimed as 'disabled' and a further four were strafed along the French coast.

1 and 3 Group spearhead

The first bomber to leave the ground from the main attacking force was Short Stirling I, W7516 'S' of 15 Squadron (3 Group) based at Wyton near Huntingdon at 2234hrs. It was being flown by the commanding officer, Wg Cdr J C Macdonald DFC, AFC and his crew, Fg Off McAuley and Sgts Burrell, Heurtley, Rose, Spenceley and McGovern and was one of a dozen being contributed. A seasoned unit, 15 Squadron reformed as a bomber unit in 1934 and progressed through the Hart, Hind, Battle, Blenheim and Wellington before re-equipping with the Stirling in April 1941 (it was only the second RAF squadron to do so). While 15 Squadron rumbled out of Wyton (it would be another 49 minutes before all twelve bombers were in the air), the first aircraft from 1 Group were taxiing out from their North Lincolnshire stations.

103 Squadron's Wellingtons based at Elsham Wolds, led by Wg Cdr J F H du Boulay were next to set course for Cologne at 2241hrs and, one minute later, 12 Squadron, led by Flt Lt A B Payne DFC and crew in Wellington II, W5361 'PH-C', began to depart Binbrook. One of the 12 Squadron machines, Wellington II, W5367, captained by Sqn Ldr P C Lemon, gained a new second pilot in the shape of Binbrook's Station Commander, Gp Capt C D C Boyce, who, like many senior officers, was determined not to miss this 'big show'. These two squadrons fielded some of the largest contributions of aircraft for this 'all-out' operation; 103 Squadron managed 19 aircraft while 12 Squadron achieved an impressive personal best by

despatching 28 Wellingtons. This was by far the most aircraft the Binbrook-based unit had managed to despatch on operations since the beginning of the war and the most fielded by a single squadron for the 'Thousand Plan'. However, this total was only achieved when the commanding officer, Wg Cdr R C Collard, promoted a number of second pilots to captains. The squadron would however pay the price for this and the toll began early when one of those new captains, 22-year old Sgt George Hamilton Everatt and crew in Wellington II, Z8598 'PH-B' smashed into the ground and exploded at Sutton Court Plantation; the crew of five stood no chance.

At Marham, 218 Squadron responded to the call by detailing 19 Stirlings to the operation, most likely motivated by the fact that the AOC of 3 Group, Air Vice Marshal J E A Baldwin, would be joining them. Harris frowned upon the idea of his officers flying on operations and was never happy when a group captain took part, let alone an air officer. Baldwin would get a ringside seat as the raid unfolded in Stirling I, W7530 'Q' being flown by 218 Squadron's commanding officer, Wg Cdr P D Holder, DFC. The entire unit's Stirlings, led by Fg Off Allen and crew in N6077 'V' at 2255hrs, departed Marham safely, with one exception. All seemed well as Sgt S G Falconer and crew rumbled down the runway at 2350hrs, but moments after take-off the bomber bounced hard and the port main wheel was ripped off and continued its own journey across the airfield until it encountered the boundary. Undeterred, what was left of the bomber's undercarriage was part-retracted and Falconer set course for Cologne clearly in no mood to miss the biggest RAF show of the war so far.

The second wave of intruders

Averaging more than 50mph faster than the bombers, the first of the 11 Group intruders departed Bradwell Bay at 2244hrs in the shape of Douglas Boston IIIs of 418 (City of Edmonton) Squadron. Led by Wg Cdr A E Saunders and crew, a formation of four and five bombers were tasked with bombing the night fighter stations at Leeuwarden and Soesterberg respectively. Earlier in the day eight Boston IIIs from 23 Squadron arrived from Ford and, at 2253hrs, these aircraft also took off from Bradwell Bay, bound for the night fighter airfields at Schiphol and Deelen, led by Wg Cdr Hoare. Two further 23 Squadron Bostons took off later for patrols over the enemy airfields at Evreux and St André.

23 Squadron's other Forward Operating Base for this operation was Manston and it was here that ten Douglas Havoc Is, led by Sqn Ldr Brown, began to depart from 2259hrs. Loaded with a pair of 250lb and a dozen 40lb bombs apiece (with one exception which carried a single 250lb and 18 x 40lb), the Havocs split into two formations of five and set course for airfields at Eindhoven and Gilze-Rijen.

The Thousand Bomber Raids

Douglas Boston IIIs of 418 'City of Edmonton' Squadron taxi out for a daylight operation from Bradwell Bay just prior to their intruder operation in support of Operation Millennium.

With the exception of Wg Cdr Saunders' aircraft, three of the first wave of 418 (City of Edmonton) Squadron Bostons targeting Leeuwarden found the enemy airfield. Plt Off Lukas (USA) and crew dropped four 250lb bombs from 1,500ft across the airfield while Plt Off G E Williams bombed in a shallow dive and dropped 24 x 40lb instantaneous bombs across the north eastern side of the target. Plt Off Venables and crew dropped a further 18 x 40lb bombs across the intersection of the runways while Sgt H C Craft and crew attacked from 6,000ft with a quartet of 250lb bombs. All five aircraft landed safely back at Bradwell Bay, although Plt Off Williams on the last leg of his homeward journey received some unwelcome attention from 'friendly guns' at Fort Roughs.

The second wave of five 418 Squadron Bostons, led by Fg Off Van Riel and crew, all found their allocated target of Soesterberg airfield. Fg Off Van Riel planted four 250lb bombs across the centre of the airfield followed by Plt Off P K White and crew who dropped 24 x 40lb bombs from 4,000ft. Sgt Stone and crew attacked in a dive from 7,500ft to 4,500ft at which point they released their four 250lb bombs across the middle of the airfield followed by Fg Off R L Caldwell and crew who attacked in level flight from 5,000ft, releasing another 24 x 40lb bombs on or near the NW/SE runway. Sgt Craft and crew completed this successful wave of attacks by delivering four more 250lb bombs from 6,000ft. Out of all nine Bostons taking part in this operation, only Plt Off White's aircraft was stalked on the way to the target by two pairs of night fighters at 6,000ft but these were evaded by 'weaving and changing height violently'; all five safely landed at Bradwell Bay.

Loaded with a single 250lb and 15 x 40lb bombs, Wg Cdr Hoare and crew of 23 Squadron had little difficulty finding their allocated target of Deelen airfield. The bombs dropped by the Boston IIIs exploded on or near a runway intersection and there, an uneventful trip for the Commanding Officer ended. It was a different story for 21-year old Plt Off R D Pegram and crew in Boston III, W8374 'YP-S' which was the only other aircraft instructed to attack Deelen. It is not known exactly what happened but we do know that it must have been in the vicinity of Deelen as the two crew who were killed, Pegram and Observer, Flt Sgt T Rankin, are buried in Arnhem (Moscowa) General Cemetery located just five miles south of the target. On top of that, Ofw Heinz Strüning of E./NJG2 claimed a 'Boston' shot down at 0027hrs; his 14th victory. Strüning's own luck would hold until December 24, 1944 when he was brought down by a 157 Squadron Mosquito. The gunner of W8374, Sgt E W Nightingale, survived with wounds to become a POW.

23 Squadron continued its attack when four Boston IIIs headed towards Schiphol. Plt Off F P Coventry and crew were not given the opportunity to bomb the target because they had become entangled in an area of heavy flak and searchlights south of Amsterdam and were forced to return home with their load intact. Flt Sgt Hawkins and crew did manage to drop four 250lb bombs across the southern part of the airfield while Plt Off Williamson and crew delivered a pair of 250lb and nine of the dozen 40lb bombs as a trio failed to release. Finally, Sqn Ldr Salusbury-Hughes and crew dropped their full load of two 250lb and 12 x 40lb bombs across the south western area of the airfield before returning safely home.

Five Havoc Is of 23 Squadron, led by Sqn Ldr Brown and crew, were the next to strike Eindhoven airfield. Only three out of the five managed to attack; Flt Lt S Reymer and crew and Plt Off P W Stokes and crew were unable to locate the enemy airfield. However, Sqn Ldr Brown, Plt Off McUlloch and Sgt Williams and crew all hit the airfield with a pair of 250lb and 12 x 40lb bombs; all five returned safely home to Manston.

The final wave of five more Havoc Is from 23 Squadron all located and bombed the enemy airfield at Gilze-Rijen with two 250lb and 12 x 40lb bombs. Sqn Ldr Cox reported seeing a large burst in the target area and large fires started on or very near the airfield, which could have been a last ditch attempt to create a decoy.

The Thousand Bomber Raids

Several of the intruder crews had reported seeing enemy night fighters at a distance although Sgt Madge had a closer encounter with a Bf 110 which they managed to evade at 3,000ft near Haamstede. Plt Off S F Offord also reported a burst in the target area and saw an Bf 110 pass overhead without engaging. On paper, the intruder operations against the Luftwaffe's relevant night fighter stations had been successful; only time would tell how much disruption had been actually caused.

The first of 5 Group

While the machines of 3 Group steadily climbed to altitude from their East Anglian airfields, the bombers of 5 Group prepared to join the fray, led at 2250hrs by a Manchester of 49 Squadron operating out of Scampton. The first of 13 detailed was L7287 with Flt Lt Paramore, DFC at the controls but a typical scenario quickly developed as one of the Vulture-powered bombers became unserviceable just before take-off. It was not long before the squadron was reduced in strength further when Plt Off Perry and crew in Manchester I, L7524 experienced excessive vibration and the bomber began to lose height. After just 45 minutes in the air, Perry had no alternative but to force land successfully, at Docking at 2350hrs.

83 Squadron at Scampton was typical of a 'mid-conversion' unit taking part in Operation Millennium. *The squadron fielded a 'mixed bag' of the outgoing Manchester and the incoming Lancaster.* RAF Scampton Heritage Centre

49 Squadron's sister unit at Scampton was 83 Squadron; they had both moved to the station on March 14, 1938, initially with the Hawker Hind and then with the Hampden in late 1938. Both units then received the much maligned Manchester in late 1941 and early 1942. At the time of this operation, 83 Squadron was transitioning to the Lancaster while 49 Squadron was not far behind. As such, 83 Squadron fielded a 'mixed bag' of Lancasters and Manchesters for this raid, some of the latter were very tired machines borrowed from 49 CF. The first 83 Squadron machine to take off from Scampton bound for Cologne was Manchester I, L7293 with Flt Sgt Marchant at the controls at 2342hrs. The first of the squadron's Lancasters departed Scampton at 2353hrs in the hands of Sqn Ldr R Hilton, loaded with one 4,000lb HC bomb and 720 x 4lb IBs. Meanwhile, the Manchester force continued to lose its effectiveness when Plt Off J Hodgson in 83 Squadron Manchester I, L7293 lost power, forcing him to jettison the 112 x 30lb IBs on board and make an early return to Scampton. It was a similar story for Plt Off A J F Rayment and crew in their 'borrowed' 49 CF Manchester when engine problems began over the Dutch coast. Again, the bomb load was jettisoned, well 88 of the 112 x 30lb IBs at least before they returned to Scampton, none the worse for wear.

Another 5 Group unit which was still operating the Manchester in healthy numbers but was also re-equipping with the Lancaster was 50 Squadron, stationed at Skellingthorpe. For this operation, 50 Squadron fielded 15 Manchesters which included a pair of 106 CF machines on loan. First away for 50 Squadron was Sgt P M Crampton and crew in Manchester I, L7460 at 2257hrs and all behind appeared to get away fine. However, it was a short operation for Sgt Weber and crew in L7471 as intercom failure and 'severe buffeting of the tail' forced an 'early bath' while their colleagues headed for Cologne.

Within two minutes of each other, the first Hampden units took to the air in the shape of 420 (Snowy Owl) Squadron, RCAF at Waddington at 2257hrs led by Wg Cdr D A R Bradshaw followed by 408 (Goose) Squadron, RCAF at Balderton with Plt Off Taylor and crew in AT164 leading the way at 2259hrs.

The final wave of heavies

4 Group, with its airfields concentrated in Yorkshire, was the final batch of bombers to take-off, beginning with 78 Squadron at Croft which had detailed 22 aircraft for this operation, led away by Sqn Ldr Kirkpatrick and crew in Halifax II, W1062 at 2306hrs. Next up was another Halifax unit, 10 Squadron, operating out of Leeming which saw the first of another 22 aircraft detailed led by Sgt Allen and crew in Halifax II, R9493 'E' at 2315hrs.

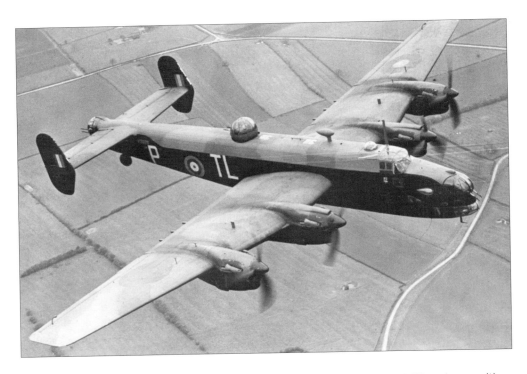

35 Squadron Halifax II, W7676 'P' which took part in Operation Millennium*, with Fg Off Lane at the controls. The bomber returned safely to Linton-on-Ouse after a 5 hour, 41-minute round trip.*

The only Wellington unit contributed by 4 Group was that of 158 Squadron, under the command of Wg Cdr P Stevens DFC, stationed at Driffield. The unit was reformed at Driffield in February 1942 from the remnants of 104 Squadron which had been posted to Malta the previous October. 158 Squadron's contribution was just nine Wellington IIs led by the experienced and popular Kiwi, Sqn Ldr D J Harkness DFC, who lifted his Merlin-powered bomber, Z8577 'T' from Driffield at 2319hrs.

Two minutes later, the most northerly located unit, 76 Squadron at Middleton St George, despatched the first of its contribution of 21 Halifaxes, two were supplied by 35 Sqn CF, led by the commanding officer, Wg Cdr Young DFC in Halifax II, L9617 'Y' at 2321hrs. A further two minutes later saw the first of 22 Halifaxes from 35 Squadron stationed at Linton-on-Ouse also take to the air in the hands of Sqn Ldr Franklin and crew in Halifax II, R9381 'Q'. Again this healthy number despatched by 35 Squadron was bolstered by four aircraft from 35 Sqn CF, although one machine failed to become airborne while the remaining 21 set course for Cologne.

Dalton-based 102 Squadron were next at 2330hrs when Sgt E G Newell in Halifax II, R9529 was the first of 20 bombers detailed to take off and, once again, a number made up by a pair of 102 Sqn CF machines. One minute later, it was the turn of 405 (Vancouver) Squadron which was led away from Pocklington by Sgt West and crew in Halifax II, W1097 'P' and the first of 19 aircraft detailed (although only 15 actually took off).

Making up the numbers for 4 Group were a further 13 Halifaxes detailed by 1652 CU at Marston Moor and a total of nine Whitleys detailed by 1502 BATF, 1484 Flt (TT&G) and HQ 4 Group, all stationed at Driffield. This typical attempt by each group to put up a maximum effort always resulted in just a handful actually contributing and, in the case of this group of Whitleys, seven of the eight from the two flights took off and four of them returned early while the HQ 4 Group aircraft never even started their engines.

Victims of the first hurdle

As this vast force clambered into the air, it would be inevitable that a proportion would have to turn back, while others would plough on doggedly and pay the ultimate price for mechanical failure. Before the raid had even begun, 90 bombers had been forced to turn back with the usual problems ranging from engine troubles, hydraulic issues, turret and intercom failures and the vast majority of these harshly nicknamed 'boomerangs' were thoroughly justified in ensuring that the crew would live to fight another day. Some captains would turn back in a heartbeat if one of the crew reported a problem while others would keep going even if an engine had failed. Success or failure, life or death was ultimately the decision of the captain of the aircraft while luck would be the overriding factor when it came to whether you have been picked out by a determined night fighter for destruction.

The Freya radar system was already registering a large gathering of aircraft over the English coast and the defences of major targets across Germany would have been on high alert, although those in and around Cologne at this point would have had no idea that it was their turn again tonight.

For those aircraft taking part from 4 Group, the climb to altitude had been an arduous task as issues with ice began to take hold. For Sqn Ldr Harkness, the problem of ice was significant as he could only get his 158 Squadron Wellington II, Z8577 to a height of 10,000ft which was perilously low. However, Harkness, a New Zealander serving with the RAF, unlike several others, refused to turn back and, as a result, the Wellington was quickly picked out by a pair of searchlights as it crossed the Dutch coast south of Rotterdam. Simultaneously, the Wellington was spotted by a pair of patrolling night fighters over the Easter Scheldt. Both fighters pounced and, within seconds, the bomber was in flames, plunging earth bound before crashing into the Oosterschelde near Shelphoek; the first victims of direct enemy action during this operation had been clinically achieved by the enemy. Of the five crew, the bodies of Plt Off A R Edgar DFM, Plt Off A R Radcliffe, Sgt H Mercer and Flt Lt B J Lovett were washed ashore during the coming days while Harkness remained missing giving some false hope that he may have escaped the burning bomber. The body of Sqn Ldr Don Joseph Harkness DFC of Midhurst, New Zealand was finally given up by the sea on December 31, 1942.

Hptm Dr. Horst Patuschka who, whilst flying a Junkers Ju 88C of E./NJG2, was credited with bringing down the first two Wellingtons of Operation Millennium at 0017 and 0028hrs.

The bombers of 91 Group, mainly located in the central western region of England, would also have a difficult journey as it would take up to an hour's flying time before the enemy coast was even reached. As these were all OTU machines, several suffered mechanical problems and were forced to turn back although it could have been a lot worse considering the average condition of these tired aircraft. Out of the 218 bombers put up by this group, only 13 returned early which is possibly more a reflection of a lack of experience in fledgling crews missing the signs of when that decision should be made to return home early. The first OTU aircraft to be lost was one which had taken off from the most westerly station involved, which was Pershore in Worcestershire; the home of 23 OTU. One of the 19 bombers detailed by the OTU for this operation was Wellington IC, N2851 '-F3' flown by Sgt W R C Johnson RCAF. N2851, unlike many others that were handed down to OTUs, had not served with an operational unit and in this case the bomber had previously flown with 2 RFU and the BDU; both of which were training units. With this service history, N2851 would, most likely, have been one of the better Wellingtons serving with 23 OTU but this did not help Johnson and his crew of two Australians and two

Englishmen as they approached the Dutch coast in a similar position to that of Harkness. The same fighters which had brought down the 158 Squadron machine now turned their attention to Johnson and his crew, who were clinically despatched over Gravendeel at 0010hrs, having been in the air for just 58 minutes. The out-of-control bomber was witnessed by many on the ground and it was not long before local services, including a doctor, arrived at the grim scene. Loaded with incendiaries, the Wellington was ablaze, while a half-opened parachute revealed the location of the lifeless body of Johnson nearby. There was no sign of the remaining four crew; the Germans immediately presumed they had escaped the burning bomber and fled. However, when daylight broke the next morning, the rear fuselage of the Wellington was found approximately 200 yards from the burnt out hulk of the bomber, complete with the rear turret and the body of Sgt R A Brookbank, RAAF. Eventually, the Wellington burnt itself out and a final sift of the wreckage revealed the remains, which included the three identity discs of the rest of the crew, Sgts J Donn-Patterson RAAF, M L Glenton-Wright RAAF and G F Bolton.

Both of these early casualties were most likely brought down by a Ju 88C of E./NJG2 being flown by Hptm Dr. Horst Patuschka as he is credited with bringing down the first two Wellingtons of this raid at 0017 and 0028hrs. These were Patuschka's second and third victories.

First 'bombs away'

Meanwhile, the bombers of 3 Group were making good progress although, as they steadily approached the target, there was much concern as the predicted break in a solid overcast was yet to appear. However, just like the Meteorological Office 'boffins' had predicted, the cloud suddenly came to end approximately 60 miles from Cologne and the ground exposed itself, bathed in moonlight.

At the head of this colossal stream of bombers was 15 Squadron's commanding officer, Wg Cdr Macdonald and crew in Stirling I, W7516 'S' in close company with Sqn Ldr Gilmour and crew in N3707 'N'. Both bombers were flying due west towards Cologne at over 15,000ft but, like all other 3 Group machines, they were briefed to approach from the north with their aiming point located at the *Neumarkt* in the centre of the old town, one mile west of the Hindenburg Bridge. Realising that it was considerably more important to fix their position, Macdonald and Gilmour instead flew towards the instantly recognisable S-bend in the Rhine, south of the city, and then turned north, making sure the river remained on their starboard side. Ahead of them lay Cologne, exposed under a full moon, all of its features crystal clear, even from over 15,000ft, the most vivid of them being the cathedral. The two

The 'office' of a 15 Squadron Short Stirling at Wyton in 1942. It was a Stirling from this same unit which dropped the first bombs on Cologne at 0047hrs on May 31, 1942.

bridges, Hindenburg and Hohenzollern, provided a final fix as if to clarify that they were undoubtedly in the right position, albeit eight minutes early. This factor seemed unimportant as the formidable defences of this city, which had already been attacked 106 times before, had yet to awaken and there seemed no reason to aggravate this situation. At 0047hrs, Macdonald and Gilmour released their bomb loads of 4lb and 30lb IBs accurately across the *Neumarkt*; it was now up to the hundreds following to deliver their deadly cargoes with the same accuracy.

As the 15 Squadron bombers began to head for home, they noticed a number of decoy fires suddenly spark up around the city. It was crucial that the IBs dropped by 15 Squadron caught fire as quickly as possible otherwise the effect of the decoys would confuse the remaining crews and the bombs would fall harmlessly into open fields rather than where they were intended. The Wellingtons of 9 Squadron were quick to replicate 15 Squadron's accuracy and, within minutes, the fires began to spread quickly across the *Neumarkt* and, in response, the local defences awoke. Every flak gun seemed to come alive at once around the city and the bombers began to fall, spiralling in flames with no chance of recovery and only the vain hope that black specks, complete with chutes, would emerge.

While 3 Group began to pile on the pressure, a few bombers from 1 Group arrived early and, rather than risk a circuit of the city, dropped their bomb loads and departed as quickly as possible. Already, the flak defences, despite their experience and organisation, were beginning to show signs of confusion and, while there was a lot of lethal metal being flung into the air, it seemed more haphazard than usual. On the occasions when the searchlights and anti-aircraft guns worked well together, the victim coned by searchlights was clinically brought down but, as the raid progressed, this happened less and less.

On the ground, the sound of hundreds of anti-aircraft guns opening up simultaneously would have been reassuring and the hardened civilian was, by now, not even in a rush to go to a shelter as many raids had come and gone and even more had just sailed on by to a target deeper in Germany. However, even the most blasé civilian would have come to realise that this raid was different; never had so many engines been heard before and the fact that the sky over Cologne was clear indicated that the city was in for a rough ride. Nonchalance began to turn into fear and panic as people began to quicken their pace and head for the large communal shelters deep in the bowels in the city. As they made their way, many picked up the pieces of paper which were fluttering along the streets; on it were written, in block capitals, 'The offensive of the R.A.F. in its new form has begun.'

A busy sky

As the bombers began homing in on their target, an increasing tendency to disregard the details of the briefing began to creep in as crews simply focussed on hitting Cologne and getting out as fast as possible. As a result, the huge bomber force began to converge on the target rather than approach in a more disciplined squadron by squadron, group by group approach. This individual approach was how bomber crews had been flying operations from the beginning of the war and, for many, this was a hard habit to break. This resulted in a lot of aircraft approaching the target area all at once and the biggest fear, which was well above flak and fighter attack, was the risk of an air-to-air collision. The planners had already predicted that a number of bombers would be lost in this way but, incredibly, only one such incident occurred over the target and this was witnessed by 408 Squadron pilot, Flt Lt B Frow in Hampden I, AT227.

With just over 20 miles to go before arriving over Cologne, Frow suddenly became aware of the number of aircraft all around him and, as the presence of flak and enemy night fighters began to increase, his mind was still more focussed on not

A Short Stirling I of 218 Squadron at Marham prepares to receive a load of SBC (Small Bomb Containers) filled with incendiaries. A total of 7,516 x 30lb and 456,231 incendiary bombs were dropped on Cologne during Millennium.

colliding with another bomber. While other aircraft weaved around to avoid the danger from below, Frow stuck to flying straight and level and warned his crew to keep a good look-out. Even when he spotted a burst of tracer no more than half a mile ahead, he stuck to his course while others around began to twitch and float around him. The effect of that tracer was a sudden bright glow as a victim of a night fighter headed steadily for the ground.

After this incident, just past Mönchengladbach, Frow spotted a couple of bombers to his starboard which were positioned uncomfortably close, one above the other, a Stirling on top and a Wellington below. The Wellington continued to weave below the Stirling and then, within seconds, rise just a few feet too high causing the propellers of the bomber, Hercules engines to slice into the rear fuselage of the bomber above. The tail of the Stirling was sliced away as the two bombers, temporarily locked together, rose up as one before separating into a dive from which neither would recover. Seconds later the Wellington, Mk III X3670 'SR-F', of 101 Squadron, flown by Plt Off A De F Gardner and crew, exploded in a violent flash, giving all five airmen on board no chance of survival. Meanwhile, the Stirling, Mk I W7534 'BU-E', of 214 Squadron with Plt Off H Dent at controls continued towards the ground with Frow watching for as long as he could before he lost sight of the crippled bomber. Frow saw no parachutes appear and another explosion marked the moment that Dent and his seven crew all perished.

Frow went on to reach Cologne, drop 360 x 4lb IBs from 10,000ft at 0100hrs and then return safely to Balderton at 0410hrs, none the worse for wear. In the meantime, the first wave of bombers had got through relatively unscathed, although 9 Squadron had lost two Wellingtons, one owing to shortage of fuel, the other to a night fighter, as well as the two bombers from 101 and 214 Squadrons that Frow had seen collide *en route*. The crew of a second Wellington from 101 Squadron was forced to bail out through engine problems and 218 Squadron lost a Stirling to flak. In Cologne, the heavy shower of incendiaries at its heart was now beginning to take effect although the initially disorganised response by the city's defences appeared to have rallied, while the defending night fighters began to realise how rich the pickings were becoming as bomber after bomber continued to stream towards Cologne. It was now up to the next wave of medium bombers; the Wellingtons, Hampdens, Manchesters and Whitleys to maintain the accuracy of the raid which already had the potential to devastate this city.

Height is your friend

The Avro Manchester gained a poor reputation almost as soon as it had entered service. The bomber, as is well known, was seriously let down by its two Rolls-Royce Vulture engines which, through a lack of development and service trials, were hopelessly unreliable in an operational environment. Thankfully, the Manchester had a relatively short service career which was mercifully aided by the arrival of its younger, four-engined sibling in the shape of the Lancaster. However, several squadrons and their men had no choice but to fly and fight in this machine and they had to step up to the plate the same as all other crews and their aircraft during this period of Bomber Command's history.

19-year-old Sgt J B Wilkie and his 50 Squadron crew were a classic example. Incidentally, 50 Squadron was a unit which was going through the process of re-equipping with the Lancaster and for this operation would be fielding two of them plus 16 Manchesters. Before Cologne had begun, Wilkie had flown to Coningsby to collect Manchester I, L7456 'ZN-T' which would be operating as one of the two

106 Squadron CF machines out of Skellingthorpe for this mammoth operation.

Wilkie took off from Skellingthorpe at 2316hrs and, from the outset, it was apparent that this Manchester was a reluctant flyer. By the time they were on the approach to Cologne, a mere altitude of 9,000ft* was reached. As he approached the sweeping searchlights, the flak began to increase in intensity and a few hundred yards ahead a bomber was brought down, forcing Wilkie to steer a different course slightly further north. The manoeuvre only brought more trouble as, within seconds, three searchlights had the Manchester in their luminous grasp, followed by the inevitable accurate flak, combined with the rattle of shrapnel along the bomber's fuselage. Wilkie did all he could to shake off the searchlights but not before the port engine was hit by a burst of flak and immediately began to splutter and emit tongues of flame. Instinctively, Wilkie feathered the Vulture and operated the engine's fire extinguisher which worked effectively but left the Manchester in a precarious position. Momentarily convinced that he could still bomb the target, reality soon took hold and the bomb load was discarded somewhere in the suburbs of Cologne. All thoughts now turned to survival. Blinded by the searchlights which continued their hold over the bomber, Wilkie turned away from the target; every input through the controls was now costing him valuable height. Despite Wilkie's belief that a Manchester could be flown over a long distance on one engine, which had been achieved by several operational pilots, this particular machine stood no chance of getting them home. There was a flicker of hope when suddenly the searchlights gave up their grip to focus on another victim. However, trying to manoeuvre away from those searchlights had forced the bomber lower and it was already down to an altitude at which Wilkie had to make the final decision to bail out. Once he gave the order, he was both surprised and slightly alarmed to see the front gunner, Sgt E W Finch walk through the cockpit and towards the rear of the aircraft rather than exiting via the front hatch, a few feet away from his station. Wilkie knew his fate was sealed because as soon as he released his foot from the left-hand rudder pedal, the bomber would flip over onto its back and plunge into the ground. The second pilot, Flt Sgt C H Tobias RCAF would also choose to remain alongside his captain who, by keeping the pressure on that pedal, gave his crew every chance of getting out, albeit at a low height. It was only when Wilkie turned on the bomber's main landing lights did it dawn him how low he actually was as the tree tops suddenly loomed. Both men who remained in the stricken Manchester braced themselves for a rough ride through the trees but instead felt the relative comfort of solid ground as the bomber slid to a rapid halt in an open area that had fortunately appeared before them. Both engines were on fire and, after unstrapping and quickly travelling through the rear fuselage to make sure everyone had obeyed the order to bail out both Wilkie and Tobias exited the bomber seemingly unscathed. Incredibly, within seconds of leaving the bomber, the two men were surrounded by Germans in Luftwaffe uniforms. Completely unintentionally, Wilkie had put the bomber down on the Luftwaffe airfield Düsseldorf-Lohausen, 25 miles NNW of Cologne. The two airmen must have had mixed feelings about their own 'good fortune' but thoughts soon quickly turned to the welfare of the rest of the crew. Over the coming days, Wilkie and Tobias were reunited with two more of the Manchester's crew which still left three unaccounted for, including Finch who had strode past Wilkie without batting an eyelid. Sadly, it turned out that Finch and two other crewmen had bailed out too low and not survived which must have left Wilkie bereft as all of these men, unbeknown to the captain, would have survived if they had stayed with the Manchester. Who could ever predict such outcomes under such stressful conditions?

Immediately behind 50 Squadron came a dozen Manchesters of 49 Squadron out of Scampton. There was meant to have been 13 aircraft but the Manchester allocated to the commanding officer, Wg Cdr G D Slee, went unserviceable. Determined not to miss the show, he immediately ran across to Flight Commander, Sqn Ldr Ward Hunt's Manchester I, L7493 and took the place of the second pilot.

It had been a period of upheaval for 49 Squadron who began the war equipped with the Hampden and then, in April 1942, converted to the Manchester which was destined to be replaced in June. Plt Off P N Floyd and some of his crew had already experienced part of this transition as they had already flown seven operations in Hampdens and been given a few days leave, only to return and find that the unit was changing to the Manchester. Prior to this operation, Floyd and crew had only experienced one leaflet and mining operation so, in Manchester I, L7290, this would be their first operation over Germany. Compared to Wilkie, Floyd's bomber would prove to be even more vulnerable to enemy fire because all he could coax out of the straining bomber was an altitude of 7,000ft. Seemingly exposed to every searchlight and flak gun in the city, Floyd found himself in the familiar position as pilot of a Manchester of deciding whether he should continue to try to outmanoeuvre the lights or dive, gain speed and hopefully fly clear. The continuous waves of flak shrapnel striking the bomber made up his mind as hydraulic lines were severed which put the turrets out of action. Surprisingly, the engines had escaped the worst of the enemy fire and, as Floyd pushed the nose of the bomber forward, their note changed and the Manchester quickly gained speed until he pulled the aircraft out at 3,000ft. This was no height for a Manchester over enemy territory let alone a heavily defended target. While the bomber had managed to escape the searchlights, at that height they were vulnerable to the lighter flak batteries and it was not long before mesmerising tracer came at them from all directions. Regardless, Floyd continued towards the target but it was only a matter of time before the Vultures would say enough is enough. It was the starboard unit that gave up first following a rise in oil temperature, combined with a stream of coolant, forcing the pilot to shut it down and feather. On one engine, and with the altitude dropping to below 3,000ft, there was only one more decision to be made and Floyd gave the order to his crew to bail out. The wireless operator, rear and mid-upper gunners made a rapid escape through the rear hatch while the second pilot, Sgt D E Randall RAAF, went down below to open the front hatch, followed by the navigator, Sgt J R McK Valentine, who paused to shake Floyd's hand and hoped that he would be following him very soon out of the aircraft. Once the second pilot and navigator climbed down to the front hatch to make their escape, they found the front gunner, Sgt J Smith, apparently frozen with fear and unable to jump. With little time to think, Valentine's brain was clearly working faster than his actions because he pulled his rip cord before he left the aircraft but, in no time, he had bundled it all up and leapt through the hatch; seconds later he was floating free, closely followed by Randall. Behind them, the Manchester suddenly rolled on its back, taking Floyd and Smith to their graves not far from Mülheim-Oberhausen. All five men who managed to get out just in time became POWs; they survived, thanks to their captain's quick decisions and his ultimate sacrifice.

---

*The 50 Squadron ORB indicates that this was nothing unusual as the whole unit attacked between 7,400ft and 10,500ft.

Manser VC

Plt Off Lesley Thomas Manser and his crew, Sgt L H Baveystock, the co-pilot, Plt Off R J Barnes, bomb-aimer, Plt Off R M Horsley, wireless operator, Sgt S E King mid-upper air gunner, Sgt A McF Mills front gunner and Sgt B W Naylor the rear gunner, were driven out to the 106 Squadron-coded 'D' for Dog in the fading light on the edge of Skellingthorpe. With a load of 1,260 4lb incendiaries, Manser started the bomber's twin Vultures, took his turn to taxi to the main runway and lifted away from Skellingthorpe at 2301hrs, at the beginning of his fourteenth operation. As Manser steadily climbed over the North Sea, the reluctant 'D' for Dog's engines began to overheat above 7,000ft. The aircraft needed to be at 17,000ft at least, over the target. The thought of being over a well-defended target so low would have caused the majority of service pilots to turn for home, though no-one would have criticised them for it. Manser decided that they stood just as good a chance as anyone else on the operation because the bulk of the flak would be aimed at the much higher-flying aircraft; a dangerous but logical theory!

Manser's logic did not play out well as 'D' for Dog approached Cologne's myriad

Fg Off Leslie Thomas Manser.

of sweeping searchlights, each of them with innumerable anti-aircraft guns in support. As the aircraft began its bomb run, the first of several searchlights picked out the unfortunate Manchester which was followed by the inevitable clatter and rattle as flak shells burst closer and closer to the bomber. With no attempt to carry out evasive action, Manser held the Manchester steady until Barnes shouted, 'Bombs gone'. 5,000lbs lighter, 'D' for Dog only felt sprightly for a few seconds as Manser tried to gain height away from the onslaught. However, a single flak shell found its mark, slamming into the rear section of the bomb bay, the subsequent explosion littering the wings and fuselage with hot shards of shrapnel. The blast of the flak had literally ripped the control column from Manser's grip but, within seconds, he was composed again. Pushing the column hard forward, Manser did everything he could to get 'D' for Dog away from the flak and searchlights but, before the bomber could escape, a wall of 20mm cannon fire had to be endured before the aircraft levelled out, a mere 800ft above the ground. It was time to consolidate the situation as the crew, in turn, updated Manser on the state of the aircraft which was on fire in the rear fuselage and was filling 'D' for Dog with smoke. The rear gunner, Sgt Naylor, had been wounded, while Plt Off Horsley and Sgt Baveystock made sure that no IBs were left in the bomb bay, to potentially fuel the fire.

Somehow, Manser managed to coax 'D' for Dog back up to 2,000ft which was the final straw for the port Vulture. It let go in spectacular fashion by bursting into flames that leapt along almost the entire span of the wing. Prior to the engine failure, the bomber was already proving difficult to handle but Manser kept the aircraft under control, simultaneously ordering Baveystock to feather the port propeller and activate the internal fire extinguisher. Mesmerised by the flames, both pilot and co-pilot calmly watched as the fire burned on ferociously and then quite miraculously burned itself out. With no chance of reaching Skellingthorpe, Manser decided to make for the emergency airfield at Manston. To stand any chance of reaching Manston, Manser ordered his crew to throw out as many removable items as possible, the majority of which disappeared down the bomber's flare chute.

However, the Manchester was notorious for its single-engine performance and the only chance that the bomber had of reaching England was altitude which it was distinctly lacking. Manser did his best to maintain a reasonable height for as long as he could but, with the bomber on the verge of stalling, he gave the order to leave the aircraft. Sgt Mills evacuated rapidly through the forward escape hatch while Plt Off Horsley helped the injured Sgt Naylor out of his turret both airmen jumped out of the main door in the rear fuselage. Plt Off Barnes and Sgt King jumped safely, leaving just Manser and Baveystock in the cockpit. Having attached his own chute, Baveystock attempted to attach a parachute to Manser's chest

Leslie Manser in a relaxed mood, possibly outside the Officers' Mess at RAF Swinderby, circa late 1941.

The shattered remains of L7301 near Bree in Belgium, in which Fg Off Leslie Manser perished on the night of May 30/31, 1942.

harness, fully aware that the bomber was only seconds away from oblivion; the brave pilot waved his co-pilot away and said, 'For God's sake, get out!'

With the bomber shaking violently, Baveystock made his escape through the forward hatch and, within seconds, before his chute had chance to fully deploy, the co-pilot was on the ground, albeit in a dyke filled with five feet of water, which undoubtedly saved his life. Above him, the crippled 'D' for Dog, rolled onto its back and plunged into the ground only yards away, taking the life of Leslie Manser with it. Those vital seconds where Manser remained at the controls saved the lives of his entire crew whilst being fully aware that he had no chance of saving himself.

The Manchester had crashed at 0200hrs into the same dyke that Baveystock found himself in three miles east of Bree in Belgium, not far from the Dutch border. All six of Manser's crew bailed out of the bomber safely but Plt Off Barnes was injured on landing and subsequently became a POW. For the remainder, they were quickly squirrelled away by several brave villagers and, within 48 hours, were being secreted in Liege. Over the coming weeks, Baveystock, Horsley, King, Mills and Naylor

Flt Lt Robert Horsley after receiving the DFC at Buckingham Palace with his proud wife on the left and mother to the right. Having served as part of Manser's crew as the wireless operator, Horsley re-trained as a pilot and later served with 617 Squadron. Crown Copyright

reached Gibraltar, via Brussels, Paris and St Jean de Luz, all of them arrived back safely in England in early October. It was then that the story of Manser's heroism was revealed and, on October 20, 1942 he was awarded a posthumous VC.

The first OTU machines join the fray

At Cottesmore, the first of 30 Hampdens, the vast majority of them and their crews seeing action for the first time, took off at 2243hrs. Only one was destined to return early, while the remaining 29 held their course direct for Cologne which, considering these were weary training machines, was pretty impressive. As part of 92 Group, these were not the only OTU Hampdens to contribute; 16 OTU stationed at Upper Heyford managed to detail 16 more, in company with 14 Wellingtons, and, again, only two aircraft had to turn back early through technical problems, which was a tribute to the hard work of the ground crews from both units.

14 OTU despatched 30 Hampdens for Operation Millennium *of which three failed to return although two of these losses were over England.*

Of the 29 Hampdens of 14 OTU, 28 were destined to bomb the target. The aircraft of Plt Off T E P Ramsey and crew, P2116 'GL-L2', near the lead of this group was one of them. Despite it being his first operation, Ramsey judged the flight towards the target as being routine but, once the edges of Cologne were reached, the expected disciplined defence seemed to be struggling under the weight of the raid. He was ordered to drop his load of incendiaries and a pair of 250lb bombs on the railway station and this was carried out just after 0100hrs, although Ramsey had no idea which of the explosions down below him were his contribution. Ramsey's navigator, Plt Off W H Gorton, gave a course which would lead them away from the target but not before they rode out some more focussed flak. All seemed well until Ramsey realised that Hampden's compass had taken them on a far too northerly route and, at approximately 0145hrs, they found themselves alone in Northern Holland. It was not long before the ventral gunner called out that there was an aircraft below them. Within seconds, that aircraft exposed itself as the source of a ferocious attack which raked the Hampden from front to back. The starboard Pegasus engine was soon engulfed in flames and the Hampden began to bank to port without an input from Ramsey. Instinctively, Ramsey shut down the starboard engine only for the port to go the same way as the attacking fighter continued to strike the Hampden with virtually every round expended. Ramsey had no choice but to shut the port engine down as well, which immediately turned the Hampden into a glider. Ramsey gave the order for his crew to bail out but heard nothing; all he could presume was that they had already departed the stricken machine. One of the failings of the Hampden was that it was not designed with fighting in mind which centres on the co-operation and communication of the crew. The pilot in a Hampden was completely on his own; there was no way another crew member could get to the cockpit from inside the aircraft. It was an isolated position at the best of times; almost a fighter pilot-like experience rather than captain of a crew. This isolation was further exaggerated for Ramsey as the flames from both engines made his small cockpit feel even more confined. It was obviously time to leave; Ramsey threw back the canopy, released his straps, stood up and took off his flying helmet. Only a few feet either side of him, the Pegasus engines continued to burn fiercely while the Hampden proceeded down in a level, yet

Oblt Manfred Meurer of St.III/NJG 1 who claimed the second victory of his career when he brought down 14 OTU Hampden I, P2216 near Deventer.

steady, flight. Ramsey leaned out onto the starboard wing into a slipstream that would be strong enough to blow him off the trailing edge of the wing and clear of the aircraft. However, just has his legs were about to clear the cockpit, the bomber pitched down slightly forcing the canopy to close and trapping his right leg. He had no choice other than to twist himself back into the cockpit, returning to his seat where he could reach back and secure the canopy before starting all over again. All this was taking time and Ramsey was completely oblivious to the fact that the ground was getting ever closer. His fiery surroundings seemed to protect him from that fear and he remained calm throughout as he once again leaned back onto the wing. Within an instant, he fell onto the wing and slid along and off into the darkness, at which point he pulled his ripcord; it was 0200hrs. Ramsey now found himself a thousand feet above the Dutch village of Diepenveen, while the Hampden continued its descent and plunged into the ground not far away. A few seconds later, he landed in a tree

Pictured here as a group captain, Leonard Cheshire was a squadron leader in command of 1652 CU at Marston Moor at the time of the first operation to Cologne. Crown Copyright

in a private back garden, a mere field away from the Hampden which was spitting flame and bullets as the heat began to take hold of what he thought was a crewless machine. Ramsey eventually extricated himself from the tree and fell asleep at the bottom of it under his parachute until he was captured the following morning. Sadly, Ramsey's navigator Gorton and his two gunners, Plt Off V E Woolnough DFM and Sgt F H Falk, were most likely killed during the onslaught by the night fighter and their remains were found the next day amongst the charred remnants of P2216. For Ramsey, the war was over; he would spend it in Stalag Luft 3 at Sagan until the end.

This was the only Hampden claimed shot by the defending Luftwaffe Night Fighter force and this is credited to Oblt Manfred Meurer of St.III/NJG 1. This was also only the second victory for this talented night fighter pilot who went on to achieve a total

Oblt Reinhold Knacke of St.I/NJG1 who, whilst flying a Bf 110, brought down Halifax II, L9605 of 1652 CU.

of 65 'kills'; all of them RAF bombers. It seems ironic that it was an RAF bomber that brought about his demise when he collided with a 15 Squadron Lancaster over Magdeburg in January 1944.

On a 'Wing' and a prayer

26 OTU was one of number of recently formed units which had been tasked with turning groups of enthusiastic airmen into professional cohesive night bomber crews capable of dealing with the rigours of operational flying. Created on January 15, 1942 at Wing and located just over four miles west of Leighton Buzzard, 26 OTU operated the usual rag-tag collection of Wellingtons which were all too often handed down to these important training units. By the time the call came to contribute to this big operation, 26 OTU only had an establishment of 27 but still managed to prepare 20 of them for the Cologne raid. For the operation, the unit would come under the control of 3 Group which would mean temporarily relocating to a brand new airfield, four miles NE of St Neots, called Graveley which was only a few miles closer, as the crow flies, to Cologne than Wing. Destined to become one of 8

Group's crucial Pathfinder airfields, up to 26 OTU's arrival, the airfield had only been used by a few 'special' units such as the Lysanders and Wellingtons of 161 Squadron which soon moved on and settled at Tempsford, a few miles down the road.

The first of 20 aircraft lifted off from Graveley's new, 2,000-yard concrete runway at 2305hrs in the hands of W/O F G Hillyer seated at the controls of Wellington IC, DV740 'EU-O' which was, unusually, a new machine built at Chester that had only served with the OTU to date. With that in mind, the Wellington climbed well and, once over the North Sea, Hillyer had already trimmed the bomber out at a comfortable 13,000ft without too much difficulty. Hillyer and his crew first saw their target glowing brightly from a distance of 70 miles away just as they had been told they would during the briefing a few hours earlier. As the Wellington closed, the searchlights began to flick around in front of the bomber until they suddenly converged on a victim. Directly ahead, a pair of searchlights joined in front of Hillyer's aircraft, almost as if it was a greeting or an entrance through which the real party would be joined. Hillyer had to make a quick decision; the right one would have been to bank hard to port or starboard to avoid the beams but, instead, he chose to try and duck underneath them. At once, he realised he had made the wrong decision as all hell broke loose and flak began to burst all around the bomber. Moments later, the port engine began to play up, forcing Hillyer to throttle it back and pitch the nose forward then, more by luck than judgement, the sudden loss of height (down to 10,000ft) shook off the searchlights and the deadly flak. The bomber was once again shrouded by the comfort of darkness but this did not last long as another searchlight managed to select Hillyer's bomber. This time, he remembered what one of his instructor's had told him back at Wing to do in this situation, 'Fly straight down the beam'. Hillyer pitched the nose of the Wellington steeply down and pulled out a few thousand feet lower, free of the powerful beam. The port engine was still running roughly but, before the final bombing run, Hillyer managed to coax the Wellington back up to 10,000ft. By this time, the bomb aimer, Plt Off A C White, had left his front turret and settled into a prone position in the nose of the Wellington ready to bomb the main railway station. The fire and smoke had virtually obliterated the city but White still managed to find his mark and release the deadly cargo onto the target. Hillyer wasted no time and turned for home at the earliest opportunity as the port engine was at the point of giving up and the bomber's airspeed had dropped to a worrying 90mph. Fuel consumption had also been disrupted by the poorly engine and it soon became apparent that they would do well to reach the Dutch coast, let alone the English. After preparing his crew for the inevitable, Hillyer caught sight of a small light coming towards the Wellington at pace; it was a German fighter! As Hillyer shouted out on the intercom, White had already returned to his front turret and was firing a burst at the approaching night fighter. Simultaneously, there was the combined sound of the Wellington's rear turret opening up and the rounds of a second night fighter attacking from the rear, rattling through the bomber. Within seconds, the bomber pitched forward, the port engine finally gave up the ghost, the rear fuselage was on fire and the cockpit filled with smoke. Hillyer gave the order to 'bail out' but heard no acknowledgements from his crew. Momentarily rooted to his seat with indecision, Hillyer came to the conclusion that there would be little point in him staying at the controls if his crew had either already left the Wellington or lay dead on their stations because of the night fighter attack. Hillyer throttled back the starboard engine to stop the bomber from spinning and, with the aircraft in a shallow, yet steepening dive, left his seat. While he was stood up in the cockpit, he noticed that the twin machine guns in the front turret were positioned sideways which meant that White was trapped inside because the power for the turret was drawn from the port engine. Hillyer immediately jumped from his seat to rescue the trapped airman and, in doing so, his ripcord caught the back of it, filling the cockpit with parachute. Undeterred, Hillyer crawled forward and grabbed hold of the turret's external release which was dubbed the 'dead man's handle'. Hindered by his own canopy and becoming increasingly tangled up in its shroud lines, Hillyer could not move the handle and, after receiving no response after banging his fist on the side the turret, presumed that White was already dead. It was now time to save himself; Hillyer gathered his parachute and lines as best he could. He swung down through the escape hatch in the nose but only half of his body would go through as the billowing canopy was blocking the rest of him from falling through the hatch. The slipstream pinned his legs to the underside of the bomber; Hillyer found himself in the bizarre position of not be able to escape or get back in the bomber. It was at this moment, when sheer panic should have set in but, instead, Hillyer experienced a few moments of peace as he thought about life, family and the young WAAF he had left at home. It was as if all the fear had departed his body and it must have been during these brief, calming few seconds when he relaxed that the parachute lines untangled from around him and he fell from the bomber. Only a few feet above the ground, Hillyer was aware that he was upside down in his parachute harness and, as he struggled to right himself, he hit the ground hard. His Wellington, DV740, had crashed near Alem in Holland and, as he had feared, his four crew were still inside, although he took some solace in the fact that they must have all been killed during the night fighter attack. Fred Hillyer was captured the next day and driven to the remains of his crew and their aircraft. He would spend the rest of the war as a POW.

While it would transpire that the OTU losses during the Cologne raid were much lower than expected, it was a rough night for 26 OTU who were one of two units which lost four bombers apiece. Out of the 15 aircrew who flew in the other three 26 OTU Wellingtons lost this night, eleven were killed, one became a POW and three were injured. The latter injuries occurred on home soil when Sgt J J Dixon in Wellington IC, DV709, was forced to make an emergency landing in a field near a flour mill at Soham at 0435hrs. The bomber overturned, killing Dixon and the rear gunner.

The other training unit to suffer similar losses was 22 OTU which lost four aircraft. In fact, their losses were even worse because, out of those 20 particular airmen who left Wellesbourne Mountford, only one, Sgt K P E Monk, survived when he managed to bail out of his Wellington to serve out his time as a POW.

It was not a completely one-sided affair and a number of OTU machines fought back against their Luftwaffe attackers. One of them was from 23 OTU, a Wellington IC, coded 'B', which was operating out of Stradishall for this raid under 3 Group control. On a course of 270° and in clear conditions at 12,000ft and at 150mph IAS, 20 miles west southwest of Overflakke, the bomber was approached by what was identified as a Ju 88. With the moon in the port quarter, the night fighter approached the bomber from the port side before turning to starboard and positioning itself on the Wellington's tail. The rear gunner spotted the enemy fighter at a distance of 500 yards but was unable to warn the pilot because the intercom had failed and, as such, no evasive action was carried out. Closing to 350 yards, the rear gunner gave the night fighter a couple of short bursts of approximately 75 rounds apiece. There was no reply from the night fighter and the rear gunner watched as his rounds entered the nose of the aircraft and then, moments later, the port wing dropped and the Junkers dropped rapidly into some cloud. The rear gunner would claim the Ju 88 as probably destroyed while the completely oblivious captain of the Wellington had no idea what was going on until the navigator lifted off his helmet and informed him!

The rear gunner of a 16 OTU Wellington out of Upper Heyford also shared in the success. Sgt H E de Mone, RCAF the rear gunner of Wellington IC, DV763 flown by Plt Off R J Robinson DFC brought down an enemy fighter during their return flight from Cologne. For de Mone, straight out of training, this was his first operation and the first time he had flown at night.

The final blow

With the exception of the 88 Stirling heavy bombers taking part in this operation, the main 'heavy' force comprised 131 Halifaxes and 73 Lancasters despatched by a dozen squadrons. This was a formidable force in its own right, so to think that this group was being employed to deliver the final crushing blow indicates that the main thrust of this operation was to literally wipe Cologne off the map.

Amongst this heavy group was also a contribution from 1652 CU stationed at Marston Moor under the command of Sqn Ldr G Leonard Cheshire. With two tours of operations with 102 and 35 Squadron under his belt, Cheshire was posted to Marston Moor in January 1942 and the chance of returning to operational flying was seized at the first opportunity. Even though 1652 CU had an establishment of 32 Halifaxes, the hard-pressed groundcrew could only manage to get 13 of them fit for operations and that was some achievement as the unit's aircraft had a reputation for being 'clapped out'. Cheshire was at the controls of the one of the first Halifaxes to take off for this raid, named 'GY-E for Edward', an aircraft that was more used to being handled by squadron pilots converting on to type. At 2344hrs, Cheshire opened the throttles and a moment later was airborne above the Yorkshire countryside once again. Cheshire embarked on this operation with some self-doubt as to how he would react in the face of the enemy, especially with a crew with which he was not familiar, unlike his previous tours of duty. However, any concerns he had harboured soon disappeared as the Halifax climbed into the darkness. In Cheshire's own words, 'As we flew across England, in the sky and on the ground there were signs of inexhaustible activity; flare-paths, aeroplanes and lights pointing out the way…' As 'E for Edward' crossed the enemy coast, Cheshire recalls, 'The sky, helped by the moon, was very light, so that stars showed only dimly and infrequently. The ground too was light, but in a curious manner mauve, so that the contrast was very beautiful. Against this pale, duck-egg blue and the greyish-mauve were silhouetted a number of small black shapes; all of them bombers, and all of them moving the same way. 134 miles ahead, and directly in their path, stretched a crimson glow; Cologne was on fire……and the main force of the attack was still to come.' As 'E for Edward' continued its approach, the fire ahead continued to grow larger until finally the bombing run began, 'When Cologne came into view beneath the port wing there was a sudden silence in the aeroplane. If what we saw below was true, Cologne was destroyed. We looked hastily at the Rhine, but there was no mistake; what we saw below was true!'

Another aircraft taking part from 1652 CU was Halifax I, L9605 'GV-Y' with Flt Lt S G Wright at the controls along with a skeleton crew of just four; two less than usual. Wright had just been posted in from 10 Squadron at Leeming and his own crew had remained behind, meaning that he literally had to scratch around for another. Taking off at 2359hrs, Wright set course for Cologne and settled for an altitude of 15,000ft which was the maximum for a Merlin-powered Mk I; well, it was for a 1652 CU one at least. All seemed well as Wright crossed the Dutch coast and continued on over Holland to a point near Venlo, close the German border, a mere 40 miles from the target which was clear for all to see. It was at this point that a distinct lack of eyes on board L9605 completely missed a German night fighter close in behind which let rip with a hail of cannon fire. The rear gunner, Sgt K J A Manley, was not given the chance to reply and was most likely killed when the night fighter opened up. Wright was equally oblivious, to what was taking place until he saw the glow of hot rounds passing the nose of the Halifax and trailing away in the distance. Once he had gathered his thoughts, Wright realised why he had not heard anything from his gunner. The attack had been concentrated to the rear of the Halifax and now neither the rudders nor elevators would respond so the bomber was soon in a precarious position. With only aileron control remaining, Wright tried to bank away from the attack but even this control surface was damaged. With few options on the table, Wright ordered his navigator, Fg Off D G Cookson, RNZAF, to jettison the bomb load and prepare to jump. Without hesitation, Cookson carried out the order and headed for the nose of the aircraft to the forward escape hatch, laying a parachute down next to his pilot as he went. Meanwhile, Wright continued to fight the control column but whatever little control he had left was now virtually gone. It was only then that Wright realised that the situation had deteriorated further as the big bomber had entered a spin; what signs of life he could see on the ground were now rotating at an ever increasing speed. Down in the nose, the three surviving crew, Fg Off Cookson and Sgts Lowman and Tavener where almost in touching distance of the escape hatch but could not prise themselves from the side of the fuselage because of the G forces being created by the spin. Unable to bring the Halifax out of this predicament by using the control surfaces, the only option left was to manage the engines in such a way that would stop the increasingly vicious rotation. As the G forces took their toll on Wright, he managed to lift his 'heavy' arms onto the throttles and then close down the port engines to idle and push the starboard engines to full power. Moments later, the spin had stop but the bomber was still heading rapidly towards the ground, having already expended nearly 10,000ft of altitude during the spin. Now feeling as though he was at least partly in control of this crippled beast, Wright evened up the power of the four Merlin engines while below him, in the nose, his remaining crew were now able to exit successfully through the forward hatch. The Halifax now took on a mind of its own and, without prompting, it bled off the speed it had gained during its descent and performed a loop with Wright now the only 'passenger' on board; he was no longer a pilot and he had to time his escape before the bomber ripped itself apart. Wright quickly strapped his parachute on, made for the escape hatch and timed the pulling of his ripcord moments after the tail of the bomber passed over his head. Seconds later, he was on the ground not far away from the wreckage of his Halifax in the village of Tegelen, two and half miles southwest of Venlo. His three crewmen had all landed safely but, despite their best efforts, were all in captivity by the morning. The lifeless body of Sgt Manley was quickly found by a Dutch civilian not long after the bomber had crashed, still sat in his turret. For the survivors, there would be many years in various prisons camps and sadly for Sgt H P Lowman, freedom would never be experienced because he was killed when Allied fighters strafed the column in which he was marching on April 19, 1945.

Wright's Halifax was brought down by Oblt Reinhold Knacke of St.I/NJG1 flying a Bf 110. This would already be Knacke's 20th victory in the defence of the Reich but his own luck would run out when, on February 3/4, 1943, his Bf 110 was shot down by a Halifax near Achterveld.

Press on regardless

At 1140hrs, Sqn Ldr James and a 'scratch' crew, made up of Flt Sgt Dewhurst and Sgts Gale and two more both named Taylor, took off from Croft in their 78 CF Halifax II, L9624 a veteran of 10 Squadron. As the bomber was rolling down the runway and, just past the point of no return, the airflow in the cockpit began to increase as the escape hatch above James' head began to lift. James immediately hollered to his second pilot to shut the hatch but just as he was reaching to close it, the slipstream won the day and the hatch was jammed firmly open with no chance of closure as the Halifax gained speed and lifted away from the runway. Despite the efforts of the crew, the hatch would not budge and James was forced to endure the roar of the wind and cold as he climbed to altitude. The crew were expecting James to turn back but this was one operation he was determined not to miss and he ploughed on. After reaching the briefed altitude of 15,000ft, the cold was already becoming unbearable and James gripped the control column with his elbows in an effort to regain some circulation in his hands. It was clear that this really was going to be struggle and, if any doubts were in James' mind with regard to the sanity of continuing in this operation, his mind would have been made up when the port outer header tank burst, forcing him to shut it down and feather the propeller. James continued for a while longer before frustratingly jettisoning his bombs 48 miles off Southwold with the glow of a burning Cologne already visible in the distance.

Ahead of him, 78 Squadron continued towards the target, including Plt Off R Plutte and crew in Halifax II, W7671. While some versions of Plutte's operation state that he bombed Cologne as planned, the 78 Squadron ORB states the following, 'Attacked Aachen 10 miles northwest of primary from 9,000ft at 0205hrs - Identified by T.R. fix visually confirmed lake'. That line throws up a number of questions in itself, including the fact that Aachen is nearly 40 miles west of Cologne? However, whatever the Plutte crew bombed or wherever it was does not change the account of the engagement with an enemy night fighter. The rear gunner, Ulsterman, Flt Sgt

The Halifax IIs of 102 Squadron took part in all three of the 'Thousand Plan' raids operating from Dalton and Topcliffe.

'Paddy' Todd briefly spotted a Ju 88 sweep above them whilst the Halifax was still over Germany before he lost it in the darkness. All eyes were on stalks and then, out of the blackness, without any hint of a warning, the Ju 88 opened fire from an optimistic 500 yards. Todd shouted to Plutte to corkscrew but, while the pilot was carrying out these evasive manoeuvres, the canny German fighter pilot kept his distance and kept on firing short bursts of accurate cannon fire. From that kind of distance, the German pilot still managed to strike the port outer and starboard engines as well as damaging the port flaps whilst just keeping distance enough between himself and Todd's four .303in machine guns in the rear and Sgt Winterbottom's pair in the mid-upper turret. The fight between the two RAF air gunners and the German fighter pilot had now become personal as both Todd and Winterbottom hunkered down ready for a fight. Winterbottom had already received a small flesh wound in the first round of action while Todd prepared for the night fighter to attack again knowing it was closing on the bomber's tail but would not reveal itself until it fired again. Then, it happened again; the Ju 88 opened up directly

The CGS at Sutton Bridge contributed a pair of Wellington ICs, very similar to this machine, which operated alongside 75 Squadron out of Feltwell; one of them failed to return. Via Alastair Goodrum

on Todd's turret and at least one round entered, shattering his reflector sight but not causing a scratch to the rear gunner. Todd held his nerve and kept the night fighter in his sights. At 300 yards, Todd gave him a short burst, almost like delivering a warning not to come any closer. At some point, Todd knew the night fighter would have to break away and when he was within 200 yards of the Halifax that's exactly what it did. It was at that moment that Todd gave the Ju 88 a five second burst causing the night fighter to fall onto its back at which point Winterbottom also opened up for good measure. The Junkers never recovered and almost everyone on board witnessed the fall of the enemy machine and the explosion when it finally hit the ground. W7671 was in a shabby state but Plutte managed to get the damaged bomber back to England on two engines but only as far as Honington where a crash landing was performed without further injury or damage to the aircraft.

It was an equally exciting trip for Sqn Ldr E D Griffiths and crew in their 102 Squadron Halifax II, R9533 'B'. A mere 15 minutes from the target there was a sudden shout over the intercom from the rear gunner, Flt Sgt O T McIlquham, when an unidentified twin-engined fighter was spotted high on the port quarter. McIlquham thought the fighter to be a Ju 88 and, after the initial sighting, Griffiths asked to be informed when the machine began turning towards them. The Ju 88 turned almost immediately and, in response, Griffiths made a sharp turn to port, forcing the night fighter to break off under the Halifax. Convinced he had shaken the

WO O Jambor flew as second pilot to Plt Off D M Johnson and crew for the Cologne operation. The CGS Wellington was shot down by a night fighter over Holland with the loss of all on board. Via Alastair Goodrum

fighter off, Griffiths returned to his original course and continued to gently weave the bomber as he had since crossing the Dutch coast. Not more than two minutes passed before McIlquham called his pilot again to say that the night fighter was back and sitting dead astern right in the sights of the rear gunner. 30 seconds later, McIlquham, his voice filled with excitement said, 'He's closing in. Here he comes.' At which point, Griffiths once again flung the Halifax to port. Next followed the rattle of machine gun fire as McIlquham let rip with his quartet of guns followed by his adrenalin-fuelled voice over the intercom, 'I've got him! He's on fire! I've got him, Skip!' Griffiths tried to swing the Halifax from side to side in an attempt to see the falling fighter but to no avail and he steadfastly continued towards the target which was successfully bombed from 11,500ft. Forgetting how busy the airspace was over Cologne, Griffiths decided to orbit the target to watch the show until he realised that he was only within a few feet of other 'heavies' traversing to and from the target both above and below. The 102 Squadron ORB also states that a second enemy fighter was damaged; whether this was also credited to McIlquham is not clear but it certainly had been a successful operation for Griffiths and his crew.

The original contribution by Flying Training Command was whittled down to a handful of Wellingtons which were destined to operate out of Feltwell alongside, or more accurately, behind 75 Squadron. The aircraft involved were a pair from the CGS at Sutton Bridge, Wellington IC, L7785 flown by Flt Sgt Geale and N2894 with Plt Off D M Johnson at the controls and a single machine of 1 AAS located at Manby, flown by Fg Off Chown and crew. Also operating from Feltwell this night was a quartet of Wellington ICs provided by 1429 Flight (Czech Operational Training); a unit already operating under 3 Group but normally stationed at nearby East Wretham. The CGS was never high on the priority list when it came to being supplied with up to date aircraft and Johnson and his 'scratch' crew were lucky to be able to take part in this operation with their old Wellington IA. First delivered to 149 Squadron before the war had even begun, N2894 went on to serve with 215 Squadron and 11 OTU before joining the CGS. Johnson also needed a couple of extra crew which were provided by Feltwell in the shape of second pilot, Czechoslovakian W/O O Jambor and navigator, Flt Lt H A C Batten. N2894 was the very last bomber to leave Feltwell at 2347hrs and the bomber duly set course for Cologne which was successfully bombed. Unfortunately, on the return flight, the bomber was picked out by Oblt Helmut Woltersdorf of 4./NJG1 and shot down at 0225hrs, crashing near Klarenbeek, three and half miles southeast of Apeldoorn. Only the rear gunner, Flt Sgt G J Waddington-Allwright, survived to become a POW.

The final bombs

The very last aircraft to attack Cologne, according to the briefing, was meant to be that of Wg Cdr Tait, the officer commanding 10 Squadron at the controls of Halifax

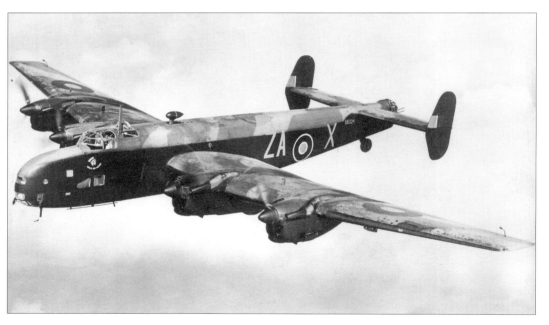

The last bombs to be dropped on Cologne were meant to be delivered by Wg Cdr Tait at the controls of 10 Squadron, Halifax II, W1052 on the 100th minute of the raid but instead were dropped on the 104th minute by Wg Cdr Lucas, the commanding officer of 78 Squadron.

De Havilland Mosquito B.IV, W4072 pictured at Hatfield before it was delivered to 105 Squadron. This aircraft became the first Mosquito to operate over German soil when it carried out the first post-raid assessment sortie during the early hours of May 31, 1942.

II, W1052 'K'. Talk of supressed and overwhelmed defences did not apply to Tait's sortie and whilst on the final bomb run a large number of searchlights were still operating and the flak was no less relenting as numerous holes in the Halifax's fuselage would confirm. With the target a mass of flames, Tait's bomb aimer, Sgt Gill, pressed the 'tit' at 0234hrs from 13,000ft and that was meant to have occurred in the 100th minute of the raid. After nearly six hours in the air, Tait carefully landed W1052 safely within the confines of the relatively small Coastal Command satellite airfield at Docking, northwest Norfolk, at 0520hrs.

78 Squadron's commanding officer, Wg Cdr A H S Lucas (who only took command on May 18), at the controls of Halifax II, V9991, had an eventful evening. Lucas had been briefed to take a number of photographs and his determination to complete this task resulted in the bomb run taking place later than planned. As a result, Lucas became the last to drop bombs on Cologne that night at 0238hrs from 14,500ft under a bright moon onto one of the few remaining 'black' areas in the midst of a world of flame below. Bombs were dropped southeast of the Marshalling Yards, although their bursts could not be confirmed despite a number of fresh fires

breaking out, contributing to the inferno below. All seemed well until, on the trip home at 0358hrs at 12,000ft, the Halifax began to ice up and, one by one, the instruments began to fail. Lucas continued to handle the situation until 0430hrs when he gave the order for his crew of five to bail out from 1,600ft. Lucas kept the bomber flying on his own until, at 0450hrs, he made a delicate belly landing on the long emergency runway at Wittering with little damage to the bomber or himself. His crew all came down near Spalding unhurt with the exception of the rear gunner Sgt E Webb who landed awkwardly and broke his neck; he died on the way to hospital. V9991 was a lucky bomber for 78 Squadron as it was repaired, later served with the CF and back on the squadron and was not SOC until late December 1945; a real survivor.

The tail enders

For many bombers, their sortie was far from over as they turned for home after attacking Cologne. It was literally a wing and a prayer for many who sought safe haven at the nearest airfield available. The risk of aerial collision over the target had been accurately predicted by the boffins at one per hour and those two incidents did happen. There was also always the risk of a collision on their return to home airfields especially if conditions were poor.

With much of England covered by a band of cloud which topped out at 2,000ft, the safest place to descend was over the vast Fens of Cambridgeshire and south Lincolnshire where the odds of hitting anything high was slim. The odds of crashing into another aircraft, even with so many of them in the air at once, was equally as slim but this theory was challenged as the first of many tentatively descended through the murk. For Plt Off G C Foers and his crew in Halifax II, W7761 of 78 Squadron, the operation had gone well. Everything had gone as planned; the target had been bombed successfully and a single package of G23 propaganda leaflets had been scattered, as briefed, over the target. Likewise, the experienced Sqn Ldr D B Falconer, who with one tour with 49 Squadron under his belt was now serving as an instructor at 14 OTU, had also had a positive operation hitting the target in his Hampden I, P5321. Unbeknown to each other, Falconer and Foers approached the Norfolk coast at around a similar time and slowly descended to a point over central Fenland where they would set the final course to their respective stations at Cottesmore and Croft, the latter 150 miles further north. It was quite logical that a number of aircraft would be taking a similar route towards The Fens as all 4 Group aircraft based in North Yorkshire had been directed via Spalding on the way out so as to concentrate the bomber stream as much as possible before it set out from the East Anglian Coast and across the North Sea. The 4 Group machines were under instruction to fly the same route on the return journey rather than being tempted to make landfall further north over the Lincolnshire or Yorkshire coasts.

One crucial difference between the two bombers' instructions was that the 78 Squadron crew were briefed to descend no lower than 3,000ft when making the turn over Spalding while it was 5,000ft on the route to the target. For the 14 OTU this would have definitely been a lower altitude as Cottesmore was only a few minutes' flying time from the Spalding area and, as such, the Hampden crew would have been readying themselves for a landing while the Halifax crew would have had nearly one hour's flying time remaining. With these factors in mind, the last thing that Falconer would be thinking about was the risk of an air-to-air collision but as he broke cloud his cockpit went strangely dark as the Halifax above descended on the same course. Seconds later, the starboard Merlin engines scythed their way through the Hampden, shredding Falconer's cockpit to such a degree that he was literally turfed out of his aircraft leaving his three crew to their fate. Without Falconer playing a hand in his own survival, his seat-type chute opened itself delivering the Hampden pilot safely to the ground. In the Halifax, the flight engineer, Sgt H Curtiss had just asked for the bomber's altitude for his log, '2,000ft' was the reply from his pilot and then all hell broke loose. There was a crunch as the two bombers met and Plt Off Foers went from a situation of calmness and control to one where he was fighting the control column and losing. The Halifax crew had no idea what had just occurred but they soon heard the order to bail out and they responded as quickly as they could. Curtiss was the only man who managed to jump out of the Halifax and even then he could see the ground closing rapidly while Foers somehow managed to keep the bomber on an even keel despite the fact that at least one of the starboard engines had detached itself. Curtiss landed hard, a mere 200 yards away from the remains of his aircraft. He ran instinctively towards the wreckage in the vain hope that he could help some of his crew mates but, on arrival, two were already dead; however, miraculously, two others were alive but with serious injuries. This just left his pilot, Foers of which there was no trace when Curtiss entered the remains of the cockpit. Looking around, Curtiss eventually spotted his captain wandering around the edge of a field with severe concussion from a serious head wound; he was alive and somehow on his feet.

For Falconer's crew, there was no chance whatsoever of surviving the collision at such a low altitude and, with their pilot ejected from the aircraft, that final line of communication had been taken away from them. Their burning Hampden was lying a couple of fields away from the Halifax, almost unnoticed as the rescue services focussed on saving those who had somehow come out of the big bomber alive. The survivors from both aircraft were taken to March police station and it was here that Sqn Ldr Falconer came across Sgt Curtiss, the officer being completely bemused as to why he was there as well. Once stories were briefly exchanged both airmen then realised that they had actually been in a collision with each other and only then did the whole situation suddenly made sense.

Post raid assessment

While bombers continued to approach the East Anglian coast, one aircraft at Horsham St Faith was being prepared for a very special operation. It was special because it would be the first time that a de Havilland Mosquito would operate against Germany and this task was allocated to 105 Squadron which re-equipped with the type in November 1941. The honour of carrying out this sortie fell to Sqn Ldr Oakeshott and Flt Sgt Hayden in Mosquito IV, W4072; the last of the very first batch of Mosquitoes build by de Havilland at Hatfield and an aircraft that was only delivered to the unit in February 1942. At 0400hrs on May 31, Oakeshott opened the throttles of the two Merlin engines and set course for Cologne. On arrival over the burning city just one hour later, Oakeshott dropped four 250lb bombs and photographed what he could despite the target being obliterated by a combination of low cloud and smoke. Back on the ground again at 0600hrs and half an hour later, a second Mosquito IV, W4064 crewed by Plt Off Kennard and Plt Off Johnson, also took off for Cologne to repeat the same sortie. Meanwhile, the results of Oakeshott's photography was already being studied and it was clear that it would be some time before the smoke subsided and the weather improved. With that in mind, sending another valuable Mosquito on the same sortie so early in the day would also return the same results. However, Kennard and Johnson were destined not to return as their Mosquito was hit by flak ten miles southwest of Antwerp. Instead of bailing out, Kennard attempted to crash land but with few options on the table was forced, instead, to ditch near the west bank of River Scheldt near Bazel. Kennard and Johnson were both killed and this was the first Mosquito to be lost in Bomber Command service.

105 Squadron also contributed a trio of Mosquitoes for ASR duties at 0730hrs but all returned without seeing anything. A third aircraft, Mosquito IV, W4065, crewed by Plt Off Costello-Brown and WO Broom, flew another sortie to Cologne at 1140hrs followed by a fourth five minutes later when Fg Off J E Houlston and Flt Sgt J Armitage took off in W4071. Both aircraft found and bombed Cologne again but conditions were so poor that no photography was taken and both Mosquitoes returned safely to Horsham St Faith at 1350hrs. A fifth and final sortie was despatched by 105 Squadron at 1730hrs, in a final effort to provide some evidence of the devastation that had been caused to Cologne. Sqn Ldr Channer and WO Jobson in Mosquito IV, W4069 flew low level (down to 60ft) without a bomb load

towards Cologne but failed to locate the shattered city because of cloud and rain; their aircraft landing at 1925hrs.

It would cost 105 Squadron another one of its precious Mosquitoes before good photographic reconnaissance of Cologne was achieved. At 1930hrs on June 1, Fg Off Pearman and Scott in Mosquito IV, W4068, tasked with carrying out High-Level bombing and photography of the target failed to return; the crew becoming POWs. A second Mosquito IV, W4065, crewed by Sgt Monaghan and Dean, also set off for Cologne at 1930hrs with the same tasking. Safely back down at Horsham St Faith at 2155hrs, only minutes after the first intruders set-out for the next stage of Harris' 'Thousand Plan'. The results of their sortie were beginning to reveal how hard Germany's fourth largest city had been hit but it would be several days before the 'fire cloud' dispersed to expose the true devastation.

Cologne – area bombing at work

For the people of Cologne, the all-clear was not sounded until 0335hrs but, more crucially, many civilian lives had been saved because of the prompt and organised response regarding the direction of the raid at the start. As early as 2353hrs, a 'Yellow' alert was sounded followed by a 'Red' alert at 2359hrs, at which point many would already be making their way to a local shelter. The main air-raid sirens

A period painting of the raid on Cologne by W Krogman.

The ruins of Cologne pictured at the end of the war dominated by the city's cathedral centre left, in front of the main railway station and to the right, the collapsed Hohenzollern Bridge.

began wailing at 0017hrs, half an hour before the first bombs fell giving the more nonchalant citizens the required motivation to take cover although none of them would have expected such a heavy raid.

Of the 1,047 bombers that took part in *Millennium*, 868 of them bombed the main target, dropping 1,455 tons of bombs. This tonnage of ordnance was recorded by the Cologne authorities as being made up of 864 HE bombs ranging from 500lb to 1,000lb of which 23 were 'duds' or delayed action bombs. 20 'aerial mines' of 4,000lb in weight and the most significant figure of approximately 110,000 'stick' incendiaries which made up around two thirds of tonnage dropped by the RAF on Cologne. The majority of German towns and cities during the Second World War were meticulous at recording the damage caused by air raids and Cologne was no exception. Property damage was listed as follows; 12,840 'residential' buildings were affected, of which 3,330 were destroyed, 2,090 were badly damaged and 7,420 were slightly damaged. Of these residential buildings, over 12,000 of them were damaged by fire, such was the effectiveness of the incendiaries dropped while the rest were damaged or destroyed by HE. Of the 'Accommodation Units' aka domestic buildings in the city, the vast majority of them flats, saw 13,010 destroyed, 6,360 badly damaged and 22,270 slightly damaged. Commercial and industrial buildings also took a battering and 1,505 were completely destroyed, 630 badly damaged and 425 slightly damaged. Many factories and industrial installations also suffered with 36 completely wiped out with a total loss of production, 70 were badly damaged with 50 to 80% loss in production and 222 received medium or slight damage with a 50% or less loss in production. On top of that, water mains were breached in 17 places, mains electric cables were damaged at 32 locations, telephone cables were damaged in a dozen places and gas mains were fractured in five.

It is with great credit to the local ARP that the casualty figures were not much higher than they were; 469 were confirmed dead. This was still a huge number of casualties and, up to this point of the war, all of the RAF raids against Cologne combined had only totalled 139 people killed and 277 injured. Of the 469, 181 were killed in shelters, 248 outside, 27 died while carrying out Civil Defence duties and 13 more were not classified. 5,027 were injured, 1,410 in the shelters, 3,114 outside, 149 on Civil Defence duty and 354 unclassified. However, the aftermath of area bombing is the disruption and displacement, especially of the civilian population, and this is what hurt Cologne most of all. The big effect came with the next batch of figures; 45,132 people were bombed out of their homes, 14,825 of them without any temporary accommodation, while approximately 20% of Cologne's population of 700,000 decided to leave the city, many of them destined never to return. The number of civilian refugees pouring out of Cologne was a major headache for the German authorities as they were a huge risk to morale across the country. While the people who lived in Cologne were in no doubt as to devastation caused by the RAF, the authorities did not want this information spread all over Germany and, as such, all evacuees were made to sign a declaration agreeing not to mention to anyone what had happened to their city.

The RAF statistics

There is no disguising the fact that this was a record-breaking raid on many levels for the RAF and not all of them good. As well as the numbers inflicted on Cologne, Bomber Command suffered their highest loss of the war so far a single operation. 41 aircraft were lost, which equated to a loss rate of 3.9%. These consisted of 29

Wellingtons, four Manchesters, three Halifaxes, two Stirlings, one Hampden, one Lancaster and one Whitley resulting in the deaths of 198 aircrew. This number includes those that died of their injuries but not those who were killed or injured in an aircraft that made it home such as the rear gunner who was killed by a bomb dropped from an aircraft flying above (the only example of this type of accident during the entire raid) or such incidents as when a 16 OTU Wellington iced up and entered a spin off the Suffolk coast; three bailed out over the sea never to be seen again while the aircraft recovered and made it home to Upper Heyford. A further 58 became POWs, ten were injured and six evaded capture. Other intriguing facts and figures show that the three main waves of bombers suffered 4.8, 4.1 and 1.9% casualties respectively which indicates that the defences of Cologne were overcome by the weight of raid. While on paper this looks to be true, there are a number of crews who bombed towards the end of raid and would testify that the searchlights and flak were still operating and scoring hits at full capacity!

With regard to the astonishing number and types of bombs dropped by the RAF that night, the figures compared well to those recorded by the Cologne authorities. Of the 868 bombers that attacked, 496 were Wellingtons, 105 Halifax, 67 Lancaster, 71 Hampden, 71 Stirling, 35 Manchester and 23 Whitley. Between these aircraft, 86 x 4,000lb (66 of them by Lancasters), 32 x 2,000lb (all Stirling), 381 x 1,000lb, 810 x 500lb, 40 x 250lb bombs were dropped plus 7,516 x 30lb and 456,231 x 4lb IBs were rained down on Cologne and all were concentrated within a few hundred acres.

Cologne Losses

RAF Losses including incidents and accident which did not result in a write-off

9 Sqn	Wellington III, X3469; Forced landing at Retie – 1 inj, 4 POW
	Wellington III, BJ674; Shot down by night fighter, Vierlingsbeek – 5+
10 Sqn	Halifax II, W1042 'ZA-T'; Shot down by night fighter, Maarheeze – 3+ 4 POW
11 OTU	Wellington IC, R1065 'KJ-Z'; FTR – 5 POW
12 OTU	Wellington IC, X9874; Ditched off Harwich – 2+ 1 DOI
12 Sqn	Wellington II, W5361 'PH-C'; Shot down by flak, Badhoevedorp – 6+
	Wellington II, Z8376; Crashed nr Düsseldorf – 5+
	Wellington II, Z8598 'PH-B'; Crashed nr Lexham – 5+
	Wellington II, Z8643; FTR – 1+ 4 POW
14 OTU	Hampden I, L4173 'GL-T2'; Crashed nr Horsham St Faith – 4+
	Hampden I, P2116 'GL-L2'; Shot down by night fighter, nr Diepenveen – 3+ 1 POW

	Hampden I, P5321 'GL-P3'; Collided with Halifax, nr March – 3+
15 OTU	Wellington IC, R1791; Shot down by night fighter, Marchienne – 3+ 1 POW 1 EVD
	Wellington II, W5586 'U'; FTR – 1+ 4 POW
22 OTU	Wellington IC, R1235 'O'; FTR – 5+
	Wellington IC, R1714; FTR – 4+ 1 POW
	Wellington IC, DV701 'P'; LWT – 5+
	Wellington IC, DV843 'Q'; Crashed at Dinteloord – 5+
23 OTU	Wellington IC, N2851 'F3'; Crashed nr Gravendeel – 5+
23 Sqn	Boston III, W8374 'YP-S'; FTR – 2+ 1 POW/Wounded
25 OTU	Wellington IC, L7802 'P'; Hit by flak over target – 6 POW
26 OTU	Wellington IC, W5704 'S'; Shot down by night fighter, Middelbeers – 5+
	Wellington IC, DV707 'D'; Shot down by night fighter, nr Venlo – 4+ 1 POW
	Wellington IC, DV709 'F'; Forced landing nr Soham – 2+ 3 inj
	Wellington IC, DV740 'EU-O'; Shot down by night fighter, Alem – 4+ 1 POW
49 CF	Manchester I, L7429; LWT – 7+
49 Sqn	Manchester I, L7290; Hit by flak, Mülheim-Oberhausen – 2+ 5 POW
57 Sqn	Wellington III, X3387; Crash landed nr Lakenheath – All safe
61 Sqn	Lancaster I, R5561; Crashed at Niederaussem – 7+
78 Sqn	Halifax II, W1013; Collided with Hampden nr March –2+ 3 inj
	Halifax II, V9991; Crash landed at Wittering – 1+
101 Sqn	Wellington III, X3670 'SR-F'; LWT – 5+
	Wellington III, Z1612 'SR-Z'; FTR – 5 POW
103 Sqn	Wellington IC, DV452; FTR – 6+
105 Sqn*	Mosquito IV, W4063; Hit by flak, crashed Bazel – 2+
	Mosquito IV, W5068**; FTR – 2 POW
106 Sqn	Manchester I, L7301 'ZN-D'; Hit by flak, crashed Bree – 1+*** 1 POW 5 EVD
	Manchester I, L7456 'ZN-T'; Crash landed Düsseldorf-Lobhausen, 3+ 4 POW
109 Sqn	Wellington IC, Z1113; FTR – 3+ 3 POW
114 Sqn	Blenheim IV, V5645 'RT-R'; FTR – 2+ 1 inj
115 Sqn	Wellington III, Z1614 'KO-R'; LWT – 5+
142 Sqn	Wellington IV, Z1208 'QT-S'; FTR – 5+
	Wellington IV, Z1209 'QT-Z'; Lost over the sea – 5+
150 Sqn	Wellington III, X3448 'JN-N'; Crashed nr Faldingworth – 6+
156 Sqn	Wellington IC, DV715; Crashed near Vorden – 5+

	Wellington III, X3598; Shot down by night fighter, Tholen – 6+
158 Sqn	Wellington II, W5392 'NP-L'; Crashed at Meiderich – 5+
	Wellington II, Z8577 'NP-T'; Shot down by night fighters, nr Schelphoek – 5+
214 Sqn	Stirling I, R9325 'BU-F'; Crashed at Stradishall – All safe
	Stirling I, W7534 'BU-E'; Crashed nr Mönchengladbach –8+
218 Sqn	Stirling I, R9311 'HA-L'; Crash landed at Marham – All safe
	Stirling I, W7502, 'HA-N'; Hit by flak, crashed Huppenbroich – 5+ 2 POW
405 Sqn	Halifax II, W7707 'LQ-K'; LWT – 7+
420 Sqn	Hampden I, AE399 'PT-P'; Crashed at Waddington – 2 inj
1502 Flt	Whitley V, Z9307 'H'; Shot down by night fighter, Hoboken – 3+ 2 POW
1652 CU	Halifax I, L9605 'GV-Y'; Crashed at Tegelen – 1+ 4 POW
CGS	Wellington IA, N2894; Shot down by night fighter, Klarenbeek – 5+ 1 POW

Post-raid assessment

**Although flown late on June 1, I have classed this loss as a result of* Millennium

***Plt Off L T Manser VC*

5

Essen

(June 1/2)

A second opportunity

With his forces in place and at least one more night where a near full moon was available, Harris decided to take advantage of the situation and hit Germany again. He still hankered to attack Hamburg which had been planned for the night of May 31/June 1 but, once again, the weather conditions were against this and, instead, the major Ruhr industrial city of Essen was chosen for the following night. Harris was so keen to hit Hamburg that he issued a personal message at 0930hrs on May 31 which was to be read out at the next crew briefing: 'By your skill, determination and courage in last night's operation you have undoubtedly struck the enemy a stunning blow. All and more that was expected of you, you have achieved. I now ask you for one additional effort tonight against an even more vital objective before the 'Thousand Plan' Force disperses and while the weather yet holds. You all know the value of a left and right and I am confident that you will bring it off.'

Up to this point, the largest force that had been despatched to Essen was 254 bombers on March 25/26, 1942. The main focus for that raid was the city's Krupps Works but a very effective decoy fire at Rheinberg managed to draw many of the attackers off. As a result, German reports claimed just five people killed, eleven injured and the destruction of a single house. As far as Bomber Command was concerned, Essen was virtually untouched and it seemed like the ideal opportunity to carry out a repeat performance of the devastation caused to the still-burning Cologne, just over 30 miles to the south.

An all-Bomber Command affair, with the exception of one machine from Flying Training Command and a similar commitment from 11 Group, Harris could 'only' muster 956 aircraft (however, if you massage the figures and factor in 2 Group's Blenheims the total reaches 1,004!) The 956 aircraft included 545 Wellingtons, 127 Halifaxes, 77 Stirlings, 74 Lancasters, 71 Hampdens, 33 Manchesters and 29 Whitleys. As with Cologne, once again the backbone of the force was provided by the trusty Wellington and a large proportion of these machines were provided by OTUs.

2 Group lead the way

As with the Cologne raid, it was the Blenheims of 2 Group who were the first off the ground for the attack on Essen. 48 aircraft from 13, 18, 114 and 614 Squadrons were detailed. The first aircraft away were 114 Squadron's 18 Blenheim IVs, beginning with V6431 'M' piloted by Flt Sgt Glen and crew who took off from West Raynham at 2140hrs bound for one of three primary targets; the night fighter airfields at Bonn-Hangelar, Twente and Vechta. These were the same targets that 114 Squadron had been allocated for the Cologne raid and the unit, led again by Wg Cdr Pollard, understood that the Luftwaffe defences would be more than ready for this return trip.

On this occasion though, the 114 Squadron crews found it much harder to find their allocated primary targets. Bonn-Hangelar, for example, was only bombed by Z6161 'Z' from 3,500ft at 0040hrs and again by V5635 'Q' from 3,000ft at 0217hrs, by which time, the resident night fighters were already mixing it up with the bombers high above. V6443 'U' failed to locate the airfield but instead chose to bomb the town of Bonn and from 4,000ft at 0051hrs hit the centre with its bomb load. 'V5455 'L' had to abandon its attack 50 miles from the English coast because of R/T failure which was later traced to a faulty valve. Flt Sgt B P L'Hirondelle, Plt Off R G Inglis and Sgt H Meakin in R3620 'A' were also allocated Bonn-Hangelar airfield but failed to return; it is not known whether or not they managed to bomb the target before they were brought down. All three now rest in the Rheinberg War Cemetery.

The airfield at Twente did not receive the attention that 114 Squadron had hoped for and only one aircraft, L8800 'C', flown by Sgt Causley and crew, managed an attack from 4,000ft at 0036hrs. The pilot of V5456 'V', Sgt Simpson, was forced to abandon his task to attack Twente at 2349hrs 'owing to indisposition of pilot'. Trapped in a cone of searchlights, Simpson was forced to dive down to 400ft to escape them and returned to West Raynham with his bombload intact. It was at a similar time that the second and final loss of the night for the squadron occurred when V6337 'D' crashed into The Channel. Sgt J L Mitchell, Sgt R M McIntosh and Sgt L A Fussey had been allocated Twente as their target (other sources claim Venlo) when their Blenheim was hit by flak. All three perished in the incident; Sgt Mitchell is buried at Rockanje General Cemetery while Sgts McIntosh and Fussey rest in Dunkerque Town Cemetery.

The raid on Vechta fared no better, although Sqn Ldr Iredale and crew in Z7356 'F' managed to bomb from 1,900ft at 0021hrs and Plt Off Coates and crew in

Sgt Gordon Shackleton (right) in the cockpit of a 114 Squadron Blenheim IV prior to an intruder operation in 1942. Promoted to pilot officer, Shackleton took part in the Cologne and Essen operations. Via the late Graham Warner

Z6043 'K' also hit the target from 1,500ft at 0041hrs. Z7761 'O' experienced heavy flak over Vechta and, instead, opted for an attack on flak positions north of Jever. The remainder of 114 Squadron carried out their attacks on Ardorf, Borkum, Hage, the railway yards at Wildeshausen and finally, Wg Cdr Pollard in V6262 'G', attempted to bomb Leeuwarden airfield but was forced to jettison his bomb load instead.

Wattisham-based 18 Squadron began the first of its operations when Plt Off R Hill in Blenheim IV, V5385 set course for Juvincourt at 2211hrs. The remaining 16 crews detailed for operations were allocated Rheine, St Trond and Venlo as their airfield targets. All five of the aircraft which flew to Rheine found their primary target without too much difficulty and all bombed the airfield. Flt Lt A K McCurdy and crew in T2331 'C' claimed to have damaged an enemy aircraft which was landing as their bombs exploded. Flt Lt F M Thorne and crew in Z7304 'T' hit at least one of the three runways while Flt Sgt J R Macdonald and crew in Z7344 'V' saw their bombs explode amongst a group of aircraft dispersals.

The attack on St Trond by six Blenheims was equally successful and all of them found the target with little trouble. All bombed between 2,000 and 3,000ft, Plt Off

Aircrew from 13 and 18 Squadron in relaxed mood at Wattisham in 1942. Via the late Graham Warner

J Whittle in V5503 'M' observed hits on one of the runways and Wg Cdr J H Newberry in Z7373 'P' reported that his bombs fell amongst a group of aircraft, one of which was left burning. All of the six Blenheims tasked to attack Venlo also found their target, although Plt Off A Breakey and crew in Z7358 'L' spent an hour searching for the airfield before it was conveniently illuminated. Finally, Plt Off R Hill in V5385, successfully located and attacked Juvincourt which was illuminated for his arrival and promptly doused after his attack. All of 18 Squadron's Blenheims were safely down at Wattisham by 0428hrs.

The first of eight Blenheims contributed by 614 Squadron to the night's offensive departed West Raynham at 2230hrs. This aircraft was Z5882 'L', flown by Sqn Ldr B R MacNamara and crew and was the only machine of the eight which was detailed to attack Bonn-Hangelar airfield. Unfortunately, the target was completely obscured by smoke from Cologne which was located over 15 miles to the north. Instead, MacNamara came upon an unknown runway, dropped his bombs and made his escape. However, just as Z5882 was approaching the Dutch coast, a Ju 88 attacked no less than three times before the Blenheim managed to shake the night fighter off without any injury to the crew or damage to the aircraft.

The remaining seven Blenheims, led by Wg Cdr R E S Skelton, were allocated the airfield at Twente. However, only four managed to locate and bomb the target. Plt Off R L Baelz in Z6173 'M', suffered heavy flak over Amsterdam and, after being coned by searchlights, decided to call it a night and dump his bombs in the sea. V5451 'R' returned early while Plt Off M E de B Porter in L1454 'P' suffered a similar experience to Baelz but was forced to near ground level to avoid the flak, by which time, the gunner, Sgt M W F Petrie reported that his turret had jammed. Porter wisely chose to return back to West Raynham. One thing that was interesting about L1454 is that it was a Blenheim I, one of only two operated by 614 Squadron. As such, this was the only example of its type to operate during the 'Thousand Bomber' raids.

The main force rises

At the exact same time, 614 Squadron were rolling down the runway. The first of the main bomber force took to the air in the shape of a 150 Squadron Wellington III out of Snaith. With Sgt Law at the controls, the bomber, X3762, was the same machine that they had taken to Cologne and was destined to see them all through their first full tour of operations. Also operating from Snaith that night was a complement of ten aircraft from 21 OTU, a unit which had remained in situ following Cologne. It was another good turn-out for 150 Squadron who despatched 18 Wellingtons while 20 OTU contributed a further ten. However, within a short space of time, three

The Kiwi aircrew of 75 (New Zealand) Squadron pose for the camera in front of one of their Vickers Wellingtons.

218 Squadron Stirling I, W7530 'Q for Queenie' was flown to Cologne by the commanding officer, Wg Cdr Holder and crew and to Essen by Sqn Ldr H J V Ashworth DFC. Unfortunately the bomber never made it to Bremen, as it was shot down by a night fighter during an operation to Emden on June 20/21, 1942. IWM (CH6310) via Tony Buttler

bombers from each unit were already back in the Snaith circuit with a variety of problems which were serious enough to convince their captains to turn back.

Unlike Cologne, even though this operation was equally well-organised, the main force did not rise group by group as you would expect with 3 Group at the front again acting as a large Pathfinder-type force. While it was 1 Group who were first to despatch their bombers, the most northerly located group to set their bombers free was 4 Group. These were the 21 Halifax IIs of 78 Squadron, led by Sqn Ldr Kirkpatrick in W1062 at 2234hrs and, six minutes later, Sqn Ldr Iveson DFC, at the controls of 76 Squadron Halifax II, W7672 'E'; 19 more followed close behind. All of the 4 Group aircraft were briefed to climb to 3,000ft, set course for Spalding, at which point the bombers should have climbed to over 5,000ft and then crossed the English coast at Southwold at approximately 12,000ft. For the residents of Spalding, life within a 'Bomber County', the sound of large numbers of bombers gaining height overheard had been nothing unusual since the beginning of the war. However, just as for Cologne the previous night, those on the ground who took notice of what was going on above must have realised that this again was no normal operation as they experienced the reverberating, chest-rumbling sound of so many bombers, noticeably under strain and pressure to gain height, heading on a south-easterly course.

The first unit from 5 Group to join the increasing number of bombers in the air was 61 Squadron at Syerston. Still in mid-conversion, the unit detailed a dozen Lancasters and four Manchesters for this operation, the first of them taking off at 2250hrs. At the same time, the first 3 Group unit, 75 Squadron at Feltwell, led by Flt Lt Ball in Wellington III, Z1570, began taking off. By 2300hrs, another two squadrons from 1 Group, three from 3 Group, one from 4 Group and one from 5 Group were all in the air, slowly gathering into another formidable force.

It was always expected that a small percentage of the bombers taking part would have to return early with various problems. At Binbrook, that situation occurred just as Flt Sgt H M Goulter was lifting 12 Squadron Wellington II, Z8431 from the runway. At that critical moment, the port Merlin engine gave out. With a single 4,000lb bomb on board, Goulter only had one option and that was to 'carefully' crash land. It is not clear whether Goulter managed to fly a circuit or put the bomber down straight ahead but, whichever occurred, the calm pilot skilfully landed the bomber back on the aerodrome without injury to his crew or a great deal of damage to the aircraft.

11 Group intruders

Once again, 11 Group would provide some intruding fighter cover but, more importantly, they would be despatching their Bostons and Havocs to bomb and harass enemy night fighter stations. First away were 418 Squadron out of Bradwell Bay, led by Plt Off A Lukas in a Boston III at 2300hrs. Eight aircraft would be taking part, four had been allocated Leeuwarden and four Deelen; the Commanding Officer, Wg Cdr Saunders, would lead the former group. It was destined not to be a successful operation for Saunders and his crew who, on crossing the Dutch coast, encountered poor visibility from 5,000ft down, in layers, to 1,000ft, all hovering

A Douglas Boston III of 418 Squadron which operated the US-built aircraft in the intruder role from November 1941 until March 1943 when it was superseded by the Mosquito.

above a thick layer of mist. This did not deter the defending flak guns in the Den Helder area from opening up, but Saunders found the conditions too poor to attack Leeuwarden so returned to Bradwell Bay with his bomb load intact. Plt Off G E Williams crossed the enemy coast north of Harlingen and, after diving through cloud from 5,500ft, picked up a canal which he recognised to be not far from the night fighter airfield. At 0032hrs, Williams attacked from a south westerly direction and dropped 21 x 40lb bombs with instantaneous nose and tail fuses across the airfield. Three bombs had hung up but bursts from those that did fall were seen by the air gunner Sgt Stuart. Plt Off H D Venables and crew had an eventful start to their operation when the Royal Navy opened fire on them 30 miles off Harwich at 2315hrs. In defence of the Royal Navy they were escorting a convoy at the time and they soon stopped firing when the colours of the day were displayed by the Boston crew. Venables continued on and, after navigating via Alkmaar, Tjeuke, Meer and a railway junction near Leeuwarden, they found the airfield. The location of the airfield was aided by some lights not properly blacked out which the Boston crew recognised to be near the perimeter tack and dispersal areas. Venables attacked from the south, dropping four 250lb bombs, with 1/40 second delays from 4,000ft at 0028hrs with no results observed. Finally, it was the turn of Plt Off Lukas who had a rough ride before finding the target. After crossing the Bergenaan Zee at 1,500ft and heading towards Marken, a number of flak guns had opened up and numerous searchlights illuminated all at once in front of the aircraft. After some very violent evasive manoeuvres, the searchlights were eventually shaken off but not before one of them had held the Boston at 3,000ft for 30 seconds. Lukas continued on to Leeuwarden and approached from 4,000ft. The target was easily identified because the visual Lorenz system was lit up like it was Christmas and at least one enemy aircraft, with lights on, was landing, although this was warned off by a red flare as Lukas approached from the northeast. Remaining at 4,000ft, Lukas dropped four 250lbs across the airfield without reply from the local defences. Williams, Venables and Lukas all brought their Bostons safely back home to Bradwell Bay.

With regard to the Deelen quartet, Sgt H C Craft and crew crossed the Dutch coast near Bergenaan Zee at midnight at 6,000ft and then turned south past Oosterdijk and Den Helder towards the target. Deelen was clear to see as its flarepath was blazing away as if it was peacetime but it was soon extinguished as Craft approached. Coming in from the northeast at 6,000ft, Craft began his bombing run and, after entering a shallow dive, dropped his four 250lb bombs at 0020hrs from 5,000ft. Flt Lt L H Wilkinson and crew crossed the Dutch coast at Ijmuiden. Moments later, an impressive display of airfield lights, complete with a flarepath and circuit lights appeared south of the town. It was clearly a decoy and Wilkson cruised over it at 3,500ft then swung north towards Apeldoorn from where he could then see the actual flarepath of Deelen in as equal splendour as the decoy. Unfortunately, the flarepath was extinguished within 30 seconds as Wilkinson's Boston approached and it took another 25 minutes to find it again. Wilkinson then began his bombing run at 6,000ft and, after entering a shallow dive, dropped his four 250lb bombs at 0047hrs from 5,000ft. Thinking that their effort had been in vain, five minutes passed before the air gunner, Flt Sgt Taylor, spotted three red flashes and flames rising up in the target area. Whilst making for the coast, Wilkinson's Boston was hit in the wing by light flak but, like his colleagues, he still managed to return to Bradwell Bay with little difficulty.

Plt Off P K White and crew had a similar experience to their commanding officer and failed to find Deelen. Instead, they returned to Bradwell Bay with a full load. Fg Off R L Caldwell crossed into enemy territory near Noorwijk but was immediately distracted by not one but two dummy airfields, one near Gravenhage and the other near Flakke. Unable to find Deelen, Caldwell steered towards Ijmuiden, dropped his four 250lb bombs on the harbour and headed for home. It was not a hugely successful operation for 418 Squadron this time but at least all of the crews were home, safe and sound.

Sqn Ldr J Brown, closely followed by Plt Off P W Stokes, was the first to take off from Manston in his 23 Squadron Havoc I at 2303hrs, bound for Gilze-Rijen airfield. 23 Squadron had detailed eleven aircraft for this operation; three Havocs would attack Gilze-Rijen; three more would patrol over Eindhoven, another would patrol over Evreux while four Boston IIIs were allocated the airfield at Juvincourt. The Boston element, led by Wg Cdr Hoare DFC, would be operating from the unit's home airfield at Ford. Like 418 Squadron, it would be a night of mixed results for 23 Squadron which began positively with a solid attack by Sqn Ldr Brown who managed to bomb Gilze-Rijen along with the two other crews who had been allocated this target. Of the three crews instructed to patrol over Eindhoven, both Flt Lt S Reymer (Polish) and Plt Off S F Offord bombed the airfield at Eindhoven, the former reporting that he had left fires behind. Plt Off McCulloch, was briefed to patrol Evreux but, as nothing was happening in the area, he chose to drop his bombs on a factory at Pont de L'Arche near Rouen. This left the four Bostons tasked with attacking Juvincourt which departed Ford at 0105hrs. Unfortunately, only Wg Cdr Hoare managed to find the enemy airfield, reporting that at least two of his bombs fell on the flarepath and on his way he also strafed a train, twice! Of the remaining three crews, Plt Off Williamson bombed Laon-Athies airfield (then the home of KG2) while Plt Off Coventry and Flt Sgt Hawkins jettisoned their bombs into the sea.

Scattered marking

It is not exactly clear which unit dropped its bombs on Essen first as not all of the squadrons recorded the time that their attack began while others were meticulous. One of the latter was 3 Group's 57 Squadron which has the earliest recorded time of 0048hrs set by WO Vanexan in Wellington III, X3331. Vanexan dropped 810 x 4lb IBs from a height of 10,400ft and only described the aiming point as a 'built up area'. Other reports from 57 Squadron crews used the phrase, 'bombs dropped in centre of target', 'target area' to a potentially more realistic 'unable to say where

Avro Lancasters taxiing from their dispersals in orderly fashion before take-off. 74 Lancasters took part in the 'Thousand Plan' to Essen.

bombs dropped' which was recorded by Sqn Ldr Laird, the captain of X3371. Sgt Davies at the controls of Wellington IC, HF915 was more confident in his report. He stated that he attacked with six 500lb and a single 1,000lb bomb at 0136hrs from just 6,000ft and backed this up by saying 'Bombs dropped on Krupps Works, seven bursts seen. Huge fire seen at the works'. Of the 19 aircraft despatched by 57 Squadron, 18 confirmed that they attacked 'a target' the only anomaly was the

14 Wellingtons of 156 Squadron took part in the Essen operation; the unit operating the Mk.IC and III for this trip. Pictured is a typical six-man crew of a Wellington III. The Pathfinder Museum

aircraft of Flt Sgt J Kormylo, Wellington IC, DV816 which failed to return. Nothing is known of this aircraft's demise other than that the entire of crew of five airmen survived to become POWs.

The next recorded unit to arrive over the target was 5 Group's 44 Squadron out of Waddington whose post-raid reporting adds another layer as to what was beginning to occur over Essen. Plt Off F Nicholson at the controls of Lancaster I, L7584 'S' was the first of 44 Squadron to drop 1,260 x 4lb IBs at 0049hrs from 18,000ft. Nicholson reported that he carried out his bombing run using T.R. and decided to ignore the flares on the ground which he claims to be eight minutes before the target. Co-incidentally, just as Nicholson bombed, another set of flares appeared on the ground very close to where the T.R. had been taken. The number of searchlights and increased pace of the flak defences appeared to indicate that they were over Essen. Nicholson's brief but informative report tells us a great deal about the standard of 'marking' carried out on this operation and would explain why the bombing was so widespread without the added complication of poor weather conditions. As well as eleven Lancasters, 44 Squadron also put up a single Manchester I, L7480 'A' with Fg Off Maudslay DFC at the controls. Maudslay describes his 'target' as 'identified by obvious industrial buildings at canal junction of Ruhr' which sounds more like Duisburg, ten miles west of Essen. Maudslay dropped his 96 x 30lb IBs into a built-up area, 300 yards south of a blazing factory on the southern bank of the canal. In contrast to Nicholson, Maudslay described the flares as 'a good guide' but there is every chance that the flares Nicholson ignored were the ones that Maudslay bombed on. Not only did the position of the target differ between crews but also the weather conditions were described between 4/10ths and 10/10th solid cloud; quite a range.

156 Squadron, another 3 Group unit, were next on the scene, beginning with Sgt Potts and crew in Wellington III, X3741 which bombed at 0050hrs from 16,000ft. Potts approached the target on T.R. and claimed to have identified the Krupp Works moments before dropping 810 x 4lb IBs. However, five minutes later, Potts reported that he was coned by searchlights over Duisburg which proved to be ineffective but throws doubt as to whether it was the Krupp Works that were attacked in the first place. 156 Squadron was also part of the 'shaker' force and out of the 14 aircraft despatched from Alconbury at least four of them were loaded with a dozen bundles of flares. Of this group, at least one, Plt Off Smith in X3339, was forced to return home with starboard engine trouble while the remainder 'bombed on flares'. As if to affirm the fact that the flares were being dropped over a wide area, Sgt G P Thomson in Wellington IC, DV812, confirmed that he saw a number of flares over Duisburg but still bombed Essen. The Wellingtons of 156 Squadron had a few scrapes with flak and fighters, both to and from the target, including Sgt Owen and crew in Wellington IC, DV799. En route, Owen was forced to jettison his bomb load two miles northwest of Mönchengladbach when a Bf 110 attacked. Closing to 100 yards, the Bf 110 opened fired with cannon which was immediately replied to by the rear gunner, Sgt Mitchell. The Wellington suffered some serious damage but, after diving to 4,000ft, Owen managed to shake off the twin-engine fighter and escape. Unfortunately, during the commotion, the wireless operator, Sgt M G McKenna bailed out and was captured while the rest of his crew flew safely home to Alconbury. Sadly, despite surviving captivity in three POW camps, the promoted WO M G McKenna was killed during an attack by RAF Typhoons on April 28, 1945.

Maximum effort

It was another successful 'maximum effort' by 76 Squadron who had managed to despatch 21 Halifax IIs for this operation, while one machine did not take off because of a failed intercom. 76 Squadron had built up a high reputation for its skill for T.R. operations and, as a result, for this trip, seven crews would make up part of the marker force led by Sqn Ldr Iveson DFC and crew in Halifax II, W7672 'MP-E'. Also selected as markers were Flt Lt Renaut in R9457 'A', Plt Off Perry in W7655 'C', Flt Lt Warner in W1018 'M', Plt Off McIntosh in R9447 'R', Plt Off Anderson in W7664 'T' and Sgt Bingham in W1045 'U'. These aircraft were briefed to drop flares only on a specific large shed within the centre of the Krupps Works complex with specific instructions to attack between 0050 and 0105hrs from a height of 16,000ft. The remainder of the squadron was instructed to bomb on these flares between 0105 and 0125hrs from a height of 14,500 to 15,000ft.

Outward bound, the 76 Squadron aircraft experienced two layers of cloud between which they all settled although the more protective lower layer inconveniently dispersed as they crossed the Dutch coast. A thin layer of cloud was reported over the target and, as the lead marker aircraft approached they saw two concentrations of flares, once again, one of them was to the west of the target and a smaller grouping to the east. Ignoring both of them, Iveson and his fellow markers claimed to have dropped their flares on target and, while there were many fires scattered all around, 76 Squadron were not convinced that any of them were the target. This would become the most accurate raid assessment so far. There appeared to have been very little opposition from flak or searchlights experienced by 76 Squadron and no night fighters were encountered as they traversed the Kammhuber Line. One squadron rear gunner did report seeing a pair of single engine machines close to the target area but, other than that, it was a quiet trip for 20 of the crews taking part. One crew that was not given the chance to contribute to the squadron debriefing was that of Sgt T R A West in Halifax II, W1064 'MP-J'. Their experience was the complete opposite to the rest of the squadron as they were singled out on the return journey by a III./NJG2 Ju 88 flown by Oblt Heinrich Prinz zu Sayn-Wittgenstein. Prior to the attack, the starboard inner engine began to vibrate and then promptly seized. It is quite possible that the three-engined Halifax slipped out of the main stream of bombers and, whilst approaching Brussels and within one of 'boxes' of the Kammhuber Line, the Ju 88 attacked. It is not fully clear what happened but the bomber crashed between the Belgian villages of Bossut-Gottechain and Grez-Doiceau, 15 miles southeast of Brussels. We can presume that Sgt West ordered his crew to bail out and that four complied while, the rear gunner, who was most likely killed during the Ju 88's attack, went down with his pilot. Two of the survivors became POWs while Sgts W J Norfolk and P Wright were lucky enough to escape captivity thanks to friendly help, namely the resistance group 'The Comet Line' (*Réseau Comète*) which operated throughout Belgium and

Andrée de Jongh, a key player in the Belgian Resistance, who helped to organise the Comet Line that helped Allied soldiers and airmen to escape into Spain and beyond.

France. Both William Norfolk and Peter Wright were quickly squirreled away from prying eyes separately by members of the resistance and they did not meet each other again until early July in Paris. It was here that Frédéric de Jongh provided the duo with French papers before the next leg of their journey which would see them led to the Spanish border and across the Pyrenees by Andrée de Jongh. In company with an escaped British soldier, the group left Paris on July 30, 1942 and, by August 2, were traversing the Pyrenees which was the eighteenth time 'Comet' had carried out this dangerous journey. They were then holed up in San Sebastian for a few days before arriving in Gibraltar on August 20 where they boarded a Royal Navy ship to arrive in Greenock six days later. The famous Andrée de Jongh, who worked closely with MI9, was credited with helping over 400 Allied soldiers and airmen to escape from Belgium until she was arrested and imprisoned in Fresnes in January 1943 followed by further incarceration in Ravensbrück and Mauthausen-Gusen concentration camps until liberation came

The ruggedness, reliability and range of the Hurricane IIC made it an ideal night intruder which operated during all three operations with 11 Group's 1 and 3 Squadrons.

in April 1945. Andrée survived the war while her father, Frédéric, who was arrested in Paris in June 1943, was executed by the Gestapo in March 1944.

It was a particularly rough operation for 78 Squadron which had followed a similar course to the target as 76 Squadron and arrived at a similar time. Of the 20 bombers despatched, 17 claimed to have dropped their bombs on the primary, which was a good average but the squadron would pay dearly by losing three of its number. It could have been four as Sqn Ldr James and crew in Halifax II, L9264, who had just dropped their bombs in the target area from 14,000ft were pounced upon by a Ju 88. Before the air gunners had the chance to traverse their guns, tracer suddenly streaked from the port quarter from a chancy distance of 600 to 700yds. Moments later, it is presumed that the same night fighter swung to the starboard quarter of the Halifax and opened up in similar fashion, luckily without finding its target and without a shot being fired from the defending bomber.

Less lucky were Sqn Ldr G D Leyland and crew in Halifax II, W7698 which collided with a night fighter at 14,000ft over Bocholt, 30 miles northwest of Essen. While the damage to the Halifax was terminal, Leyland managed to steer the crippled bomber a further ten miles north before it crashed near Winterswijk. Only Leyland and two others survived to become POWs while three others perished. This bomber was also claimed shot down by Oblt Helmut Woltersdorf of 7./NJG1 at 0208hrs. Whether Woltersdorf was flying the night fighter that hit the bomber or saw an opportunity to finish it off is open to debate. However, one thing is for sure, this would be Woltersdorf last victory.

Sgt P M Gawith, RNZAF lifted his 3 Squadron Hurricane IIC off Manston's long runway at 0030hrs, one of six fighters from that unit which would contribute to the night intruder operations. Gawith was briefed to carry out an intruder sortie against

Sgt A R Tonkin RAAF and his 214 Squadron crew boarding their Stirling I, R9326 bound for Essen. Also pictured are Flt Sgt L C Beagles and Sgts, G H Ransome, C L Honeychurch RCAF, W D Horne, G D Morton, S G Goodey and Lyle. Tonkin and his crew failed to return from a Gardening operation on June 11/12 and all became POWs with exception of Sgt Lyle who was replaced by Sgt A Ballentine.

Although presented here wearing the codes of 207 Squadron, Manchester I, L7319 was transferred to 50 Squadron. It was with this unit that Plt Off D A Atkinson and crew flew the bomber to Cologne and Essen.

Twente airfield which was found with little difficulty thanks to its lights blazing, although these were extinguished as he approached. Gawith continued on to Rheine airfield where, once again, the runway's lights were exposed for him but were doused quickly again when it was realised that his aircraft was not from Luftwaffe stock. With nothing more than some inaccurate enemy machine gun fire

for his trouble so far, Gawith set course for Manston but was distracted by a train north of Rheine which he attacked. For some reason, Gawith thought Twente was worth a second visit before he re-crossed the Channel, a decision that was destined to pay dividends. Approaching Twente, he spotted an enemy aircraft which he attacked without hesitation, scoring numerous strikes along the fuselage and wings. He then caught sight of a Ju 88 above him which he also attacked but by then he was down to his last few rounds and was forced to break off. On return to Manston at 0410hrs, Gawith only claimed one unidentified aircraft damaged but it would later come out that the first machine was that of Oblt Helmut Woltersdorf who was only minutes from landing where he would have celebrated his 15th victory. Woltersdorf and his crew were killed which was bitter sweet revenge for the two crews he had brought down during this operation. There would be no true winners from this scenario, Sgt Gawith RNZAF, DFM was killed during another night intruder operation over Holland on July 28/29, 1942.

78 Squadron also lost Plt Off J S Lawson, RCAF and crew in Halifax II, R9364 which was engaged by flak possibly *en route* to the target as the bomber crossed the Dutch coast. It is not clear if it was an evasive manoeuvre that the caused the rudders to stall or if it was as a result of being hit by flak but moments later the Halifax entered a flat spin from which it could not recover. The crew had time to signal an SOS fix 18 miles due west of The Hague before the bomber struck the sea and broke into two pieces. Two airmen, Flt Sgt T B Miller, GM, RCAF and Plt Off P J Jones were thrown into the sea on impact and, as a result, were the only survivors. After spending four days in a dinghy, both with serious injuries, they were rescued by a German boat and delivered into captivity for the remainder of the war. Finally, 78 Squadron's list of losses ended when Plt Off H G Clothier, RCAF and crew in Halifax II, W1143, which was borrowed from 10 Squadron and took off from Leeming, crashed into the Haringvliet off Hellevoetsluis. Only the Flight Engineer, Sgt W R Forbes, survived to become a POW.

By the time the lead aircraft of 10, 101, 102 and 207 Squadrons had all arrived simultaneously at 0053hrs over the target, the crews would have been presented

50 Squadron Avro Manchester I, L7476 took part in the operations to Cologne and Essen, both with Plt Off T Cole at the controls. During the Essen operation the bomber was hit by flak which injured the navigator. 50 Squadron archives

with a number of options because large fires had begun to form over an area covering at least 100 square miles! A number of dummy fires were also springing up all around the increasingly large area, some of them noted by Sqn Ldr Seymour-Price in the lead 10 Squadron bomber, Halifax II, W7678 'ZA-B'. Bombs were dropped from 16,500ft on a T.R. fix through a solid cloud layer at approximately 3,000ft. It was destined to be a rough night for 10 Squadron as well; 20 aircraft, including those from 10CF, were despatched from Leeming but only twelve claimed to have bombed the primary target. WO O'Driscoll in Halifax II, W7695, was flying one of the bombers that were forced back early owing to mechanical failure and then the attentions of a Bf 110 night fighter. Outbound, the port outer engine water temperature had begun to rise alarmingly high and then at 0030hrs, still short of the target, a Bf 110 approached from astern and fired a short burst. Obviously a cautious night fighter pilot was at the controls and one who may have experienced the sting in the tail from a Halifax in the past. Assisted by some quick evasive manoeuvres by O'Driscoll, any further attacks were thwarted. At 0044hrs, the port engine was still playing up, forcing O'Driscoll to turn for home and jettison the bomb load 20 miles off the Dutch coast before limping back to Leeming. Two 10 Squadron

A trio of 408 (Goose) Squadron, RCAF Hampden Is in formation out of Balderton in 1942. The squadron contributed to all three 'Thousand Plan' operations.

Halifaxes never made it back to Leeming, the first, Halifax II, L9623 with Plt Off E R Senior was forced to ditch off the Dutch coast. Word did not get back to the squadron until June 6 that six of the seven crew were POWs while the rear gunner Sgt J Whitfield was still missing. Halifax II, W1098 flown by Plt Off D D P Joyce RCAF and crew was the other 10 Squadron aircraft. The bomber crashed at

Oeding, 35 miles north of Essen; only the bomb aimer, Flt Sgt K R Kettlewell RCAF survived to become a POW.

Earlier that day, 101 Squadron gained a new commanding officer when Wg Cdr E C Eaton DFC took over the reins from Wg Cdr T H L Nicholls who had completed his tour of duty. As such, the unit was led by Sqn Ldr Watters for this operation and it was his aircraft, Wellington III, X3654 and that of Flt Lt Harper and crew, X3991 which were the first of 101 Squadron to arrive over the target. It would be a successful and lucky night for 101 Squadron; all ten of its Wellingtons claimed to have bombed the target and all of them, plus a further five aircraft 23 OTU, returned safely back to Bourn.

207 Squadron was the first Lancaster-equipped unit to join in the fray; Sqn Ldr K H P Beauchamp was the lead of 14 aircraft put up that night. However, four Lancasters had to return with mechanical issues; three of them related to the engines and a fourth had oxygen failure. Of the remainder, all claimed to have bombed the primary target of the Krupps Works or the secondary of Essen itself. Sqn Ldr W D B Ruth DFC and crew in Lancaster L7582 'D' was the first to attack from 18,000ft with 1,260 x 4lb IBs. Even though Ruth described the cloud cover as 10/10ths, a T.R. fix on the 'target' was confirmed visually.

Fg Off G A Ings and crew in Lancaster I, R5628 had an eventful trip which began at 0109hrs when they dropped a single 4,000lb bomb and 720 x 4lb IBs from 15,000ft in a 'built up area'. Ings later reported '…effectiveness of flares spoiled by a thin layer of cloud' while, in contrast, Sqn Ldr Ruth stated that '…flares were useful for guiding aircraft to target'. Meanwhile, Ings turned for home and over Holland was intercepted by a pair of Ju 88 night fighters. The first was shaken off without a shot being fired thanks to some good evasive manoeuvres, while the second took the Lancaster on head on. The front gunner did just enough with a short burst of fire to put the night fighter off and, to make sure that he had shaken off his pursuers, Ings dived down to 1,000ft before escaping back home.

Another Lancaster crew that were lucky to get through this operation were 83 Squadron's Fg Off R G W Oakley and crew in R5625. Whilst approaching the primary target, the Lancaster was hit by flak at 16,000ft forcing Oakley to jettison his bomb load, however, half of the 1,260 incendiaries that the Lancaster was carrying refused to leave. A quick assessment of the damage caused by the flak revealed that the port aileron had been completely shot away and the starboard one was damaged. Whether through damage or a lack of power, the instrument panel was also unreadable. It was time for some cool heads and, while Oakley and his second pilot managed to keep the bomber on an even keel, the order was given to prepare to bail out. To add to the crew's troubles, the Lancaster was held in a number of searchlights for an agonising length of time but somehow enough control

Wellington IV, Z1572 of 419 Squadron took part in the operation to Essen and Millennium II in the hands of Plt Off Jost and crew. A bomber with a charmed life, it had already served with 115 and 75 Squadrons before reaching 419 Squadron. It was then passed on to 16 OTU and was not SOC until April 30, 1945. Charles E Brown/419 Squadron Records

was maintained to shake them off. With some semblance of order returning, and through the combined efforts of the crew, the Lancaster was brought back home to Scampton without any further damage; it so easily could have been another bomber lost.

214 Squadron's Stirlings, which were not part of 'flare force' for this operation, despite being *GEE*-equipped, were next over the target at 0054hrs. Of the eleven Stirling's despatched, two of them were forced to return early, one with trouble with the negative and positive earth in the bombing circuit and the other with an unserviceable rear turret thanks to a burst hydraulic line while another bomber was forced to land away. Of the remaining eight, all claimed to have bombed the primary target between 0054 and 0134hrs from a height between 14,000 and 16,000ft. One Stirling was hit by an enthusiastic air gunner from a Wellington just after leaving the target area and decided to land at Newmarket on return rather than its home airfield of Stradishall just ten miles to the southeast; luckily there were no injuries from this 'friendly' incident which had just as much chance of occurring in a busy sky as a night fight attack did. All 214 Squadron crews found the target difficult to locate mainly because of the haze but, using a distinctive bend in the River Ruhr as a fix, claimed to have accurately bombed thanks to *GEE*.

There were a large number of searchlights positioned around Essen and the Ruhr, also known as 'Happy Valley' to the crews. A large number of searchlights were reported by crews during this particular operation although they seem to have been less co-ordinated than usual as the poor conditions were affecting their efficiency as well. However, a number did manage to find their quarry and at least three Wellingtons of 460 Squadron (RAAF) responded accordingly. The first of three incidents reported by 460 Squadron was by Plt Off J F Summers and crew in Wellington IV, Z1463 'L'. After bombing a '…built up area in the Ruhr…' at 0105hrs from 8,500ft, the crew set course for home. At 0142hrs they were picked up by a group of searchlights close to Dordrecht with at least another 30 miles to cover before they reached the relative safety of the Dutch coast and beyond. Unable to shake the determined searchlight crews off, Summers dropped down to 500ft at which point the rear gunner, Sgt T C Harris opened fire straight down the beam. The light wavered before Harris gave it a second burst for good measure and then, with the beam extinguished, its grip of the Wellington was released. Plt Off J Falkiner and crew in Z1284 'A' had a similar experience as they approached the Dutch coast near Colijnsplaat at 0244hrs. Dropping to as low as 400ft, the searchlight was attacked in similar fashion and was described as going out with a 'blue puff'. Finally, Sgt R J Buckingham and crew in Z1383 'D' were at the point of crossing the Belgian coast, three miles north of Blankenbergh, when they were coned by a number of searchlights at 0245hrs. On this occasion, Buckingham descended to 1,000ft both front and rear gunner's engaged no less than six searchlights of which at least one was put out of action.

The Hampden crews of 420 Squadron were as frustrated as those who had bombed before them with regard to locating the target. Flt Lt A P Dart summed up the general feeling in his post-raid report by saying, 'It was disappointing not to be able to definitely identify the target but it seemed fairly certain that fires of considerable magnitude were burning in the area'. 13 of the 15 Hampdens despatched by 420 Squadron, claimed to have attacked Essen rather than the Krupps Works because of low cloud.

The final stages

Of the 33 Manchesters taking part in the Essen operation, eight of them were supplied by 49 Squadron at Scampton. The unit, like so many others at the time, were transitioning to the Lancaster and one, R5850, flown by Flt Sgt Rolands, was contributed by the squadron as well. 49 Squadron's groundcrew were well versed with the trials and tribulations of the Manchester and they always had their own 'maximum effort' when it came to getting these machines ready for operations. Of the eight Manchesters, the groundcrew had managed to get all of them airborne, although two continued to play them up until the bitter end. Plt Off S T Farrington's Manchester I, L7479 did not get airborne from Scampton until 0050hrs nor did Sqn Ldr P M de Mestre's L7389 until 0056hrs; the latter 70 minutes later than planned because of engine problems. Both bombers were forced to turn back by the time they made it to the Dutch coast as neither had sufficient time to reach the target. Of the remainder, six bombers claimed to have bombed the target, even though Sgt Burton in Manchester I, L7493 bombed Cologne, while a seventh was destined not to return. The last that anything was heard of Plt Off W C Shackleton and crew in Manchester I, R5794 was at 0219hrs when an SOS signal was sent declaring that the starboard engine had become unserviceable. Not long after sending this message, the Manchester was attacked by a night fighter of 2./NJG1 flown by Fw Heinz Pähler and crashed near Voorheide, seven miles east of Turnhout. Of the seven crew only two, Sgts C D Nolan and R C Shannon RAAF, survived to become POWs. This was the only Manchester loss of the operation; the odds only improving with the type's depleting numbers as its operational days were drawing to a close.

A lone Manchester also appeared in the rank and file of 408 Squadron which was primarily a Hampden unit and was destined to re-equip with the Halifax later in the year. The Manchester that joined 408 Squadron for this operation was being flown by Sqn Ldr L B B Price who was converting to the type at Syerston at the time and, rather than missing out, he managed to 'borrow' a 61 Squadron machine for the operation. Price and his crew, like so many, bombed what he believed to be Essen through 5/10th cloud from 12,600ft before returning safely to Syerston. It was a more exciting operation for Sgt R J Fern and crew in Hampden I, AE439. As Fern approached the target he was presented with a thin layer of cloud over the general area at approximately 5,000ft. Whilst searching for the target, the Hampden was hit by flak and the crew were forced to jettison their load of 360 x 4lb IBs ten miles west northwest of Essen and made for home. It was at this point that they realised the extent of the damage to their aircraft as one bomb bay door was completely missing and the other was clinging on, trailing behind the Hampden. Luckily, no one was injured and Fern put the Hampden safely back down at Balderton with no further trouble.

Plt Off Charlton and his 408 Squadron crew in Hampden I, AT191 were not so lucky. They all perished when their aircraft was brought down by a 2./NJG2 night fighter being flown by Lt Karl-Heinz Vollkopf, into the Ijsselmeer. An experienced crew, 408 Squadron felt their loss as between the four crew they had nearly 600 operational hours between them. Wireless Operator/Air Gunner, Flt Sgt F J E Womar DFM had already completed a full tour with 144 Squadron and, in total, this was his 56th operation!

158 Squadron, who had managed to contribute nine Wellington IIs for the Cologne operation, could only scrape together seven aircraft for Essen and one of those could not take off because of a rear turret fault. The reason for this was that the squadron was only days away from departing Driffield to East Moor where it would re-equip with the Halifax II. All six of 158 Squadron's crews claimed to have bombed the target; some were adamant that they had hit the Krupps Works. Regardless, they all returned safely to Driffield while other aircrew who had been detached from 158 Squadron to bolster other units were not so lucky. Five of them failed to return including Sgts H Jackson, C R Read, J Williams and H J Daly RCAF, who had made up the crew of 1652 CU Halifax II, R9372 with Plt Off H A Williams at the controls. Whilst over Essen, the Halifax had lost power in one engine and then during the flight home over Holland, had struggled to maintain height. A night fighter took advantage of the bomber's predicament and shot it down near Ijmuiden but all six crew managed to bail out and survive as POWs. The fifth member of 158 Squadron who was detached to another unit was Sgt A B Hedger who was loaned to 10 Squadron for this operation. Hedger was one of the six survivors from the ditched L9623 and by the time he had returned to his unit they had already moved to East Moor.

During the hours leading up to this operation there was an air of routine at Hemswell as the Polish crews of 301 Squadron prepared themselves while groundcrews worked hard to get 14 Wellingtons IVs ready for another 'big op'. One of the 'routine' events taking place that day was a session of clay pigeon shooting for the air gunners and a lecture they had all attended called 'Enemy night-fighter tactics.' Two of those air gunners belonged to Fg Off D Plawski's crew, namely Sgts R Radecki and K Podgorski and that lecture would prove to be a useful refresher.

At the controls of Wellington IV, Z1331, Plawski dropped 810 x 4lb IBs from 17,000ft on what he believed to be Essen at 0155hrs through 9/10ths and 10/10th low cloud. After leaving the target, Germany and Holland were crossed without incident and, up to a point approximately 50 to 60 miles east of Harwich, it was looking to be another uneventful trip. However, the crew of a Ju 88 night fighter had a different idea when it suddenly attacked the Wellington at 0315hrs at a height of 10,000ft. Plawski responded quickly and through a number of evasive manoeuvres, including diving turns, the night fighter was outplayed. During this combat, the Ju 88 closed to within 100 yards at which point it received a burst or two from Radecki in the rear turret and when the night fighter tried to escape it took another burst from Podgorski in the front turret; both of them claimed strikes on the enemy aircraft. While the Plawski crew survived this incident to fight another day, this would be short-lived as their bomber was destined to crash into the Ijsselmeer during another operation to Essen on June 5/6.

Another Polish unit, 305 Squadron out of Lindholme managed to despatch 13 Wellington IIs; their crews having been given the blanket order '....to attack any built up area in the district.' One of the first bombers away from Lindholme was Wellington II, Z8343 'S' with Plt Off Molata at the controls. Molata bombed on ETA from 16,000ft, observing at least nine different fires down below before turning for home. On the return trip, Molata's Wellington became one of no less than five 305 Squadron bombers singled out for attacks by enemy night fighters. Z8343 was fired upon by a twin-engined night fighter from 500 yards from the 'Red Quarter to Green Beam' but luckily this was successfully evaded. Z8339 'N' was attacked by a Bf 110 and Z8425 'K' was equally lucky to escape the attentions of four enemy aircraft five miles southwest of Essen at just 500ft; all of the night fighters were reported to have had yellow lights in their noses. Z8596 'A' was attacked by a twin-engined enemy aircraft from a range of 30 yards with cannon and machine gun fire and Z8422 'V' was also attacked by a twin-engined enemy aircraft at 0130hrs but all of the 305 Squadron Wellingtons manage to outmanoeuvre and escape their attackers. It is possible that a sixth was also attacked by an enemy night fighter and damaged as a result. This was Wellington II, Z8583 'Z', being flown by Mjr R J Hirszbandt* OBE, DFC and crew, which stalled and crashed, killing all on board at Manor Farm, Billingford while trying to make a single-engined approach into Swanton Morley, Norfolk. A career, pre-war Polish Air Force pilot and test pilot, Hirszbandt received his OBE for services with 6 AACU.

*43 year-old Robert Juljusz Hirszbandt is listed as a Major (Polish Air Force rank) with the CWGC, a Flt Lt in the squadron ORB and a Wg Cdr in Bomber Command Losses 1942

The Thousand Bomber Raids

The OTUs play their part - again

91 and 92 Group pulled out all the stops for this operation again by contributing 244 aircraft from 13 of its OTUs. The majority of these aircraft were Wellingtons while the remainder was made up of 27 Hampdens from 14 OTU and 22 Whitleys supplied by 10 OTU. There were only 29 Whitleys taking part in the entire raid, the oddments being made up by Target Towing Flights. Of the Whitleys despatched by10 OTU out of Abingdon, only one turned back with technical problems while one failed to return, the only example of its type to be shot down during this raid. Sqn Ldr D B G Tomlinson DFC and crew in Whitley V, Z6581 were brought down by a 3./NJG1 night fighter flown by Hptm Alfred Haesler. The bomber crashed with the loss of all five crew just over the Dutch border near Breedenbroek, seven miles northwest of Bocholt.

The Hampdens of 14 OTU were lucky on this operation with the exception of one airman. Of the 25 Hampdens that took off from Cottesmore, 25 of them claimed to have bombed Essen. Unfortunately for one of those aircraft, one airman was killed when a 4lb IB struck his Hampden an all-too common problem when large formations bombed from different heights. 11 OTU contributed eleven aircraft, losing one of them, Wellington IC, DV767 flown by Plt Off J F Stanley and crew while 12 OTU managed to detail 20 of its Wellingtons. However, of those 20, only 13 found or attacked the target and one, Wellington IC, X3203, failed to return after it was struck by flak at 14,000ft over Essen. Four of the five crew managed to bail out to become POWs.

In contrast, 15 OTU at Harwell despatched 21 Wellingtons and all returned safely while 16 OTU despatched the most of all of the Bomber Command OTUs with 30 aircraft. This was in part achieved by the fact that the OTU was converting from the Hampden to the Wellington at the time and even by early June still had large numbers of both types available. There are few details as to how well the raid went for the unit, but after being attacked by an enemy night fighter, an air gunner in Hampden I, P2080 claimed to have shot it down in a brief exchange of fire. 16 OTU was destined only to lose one aircraft when Wellington IC, DV763 crashed at Perk, eight miles northeast of Brussels. Two were killed, the pilot, Plt Off R J Robinson DFC and his observer Fg Off C O'Brien, while two became POWs and one evaded capture. The latter was none other than rear gunner Sgt H E De Mone RCAF (now on his second operation), who had achieved early success during his first trip to Cologne. Like so many others who were fortunate enough to parachute down into occupied Belgium, De Mone was quickly hidden away by the local resistance. It was not long before he joined Plt Off R M Horsley and Sgt L H Baveystock (both from the Manser crew) who had also been helped by the network and, on the night of June 12/13, escaped across the Pyrenees and then onto Gibraltar. It was here that the Manser crew were reunited with Sgts S E King, A McF Mills and B W Naylor (the rest of the Manser crew) and on July 6 all six airmen set sail from Gibraltar.

18 OTU out of Hemswell put up eight Wellingtons but lost one, Mk IC, HF981 and its five crew while 20 OTU despatched 13 bombers and also lost one, Wellington IC, X9975 along with its six crew. 21 OTU, operating from Moreton-in-Marsh and Snaith (alongside 150 Squadron) contributed a total of 21 Wellingtons and it too lost a single bomber when Mk IC, W5618 piloted by Sgt F B Albright RCAF failed to return. 22 OTU operating out of Wellesbourne Mountford fielded a dozen Wellington ICs including X9932 'S' flown by Plt Off J Lancaster. Jo Lancaster had flown this same machine to Cologne and 'S' served him and his crew well for this operation too. Lancaster had already flown 31 operations with 40 Squadron before being posted to 22 OTU as an instructor. Later posted to 28 OTU at Wymeswold, Lancaster completed a second tour with 12 Squadron, eventually completing a total of 54 operations. He became a test pilot flying a number of exotic machines including the Armstrong Whitworth AW.52 from which he became the first pilot to eject from a British aircraft in May 1949. Lancaster did not retire until 1984 and by then he had 13,000 flying hours under his belt and as of August 2017 he is still going strong at the tender age of 98!

Of all of the OTUs taking part in the Essen raid, it was 23 OTU operating out of Pershore that was hit the hardest when two from the 14 despatched failed to return. Wellington IC, R1266 flown by Fg Off W J Mawdesley RAAF and crew came down near Kerdriel and Z8867 flown by Flt Lt W J Ewart and crew crashed near Venlo; none of the ten crew from the two aircraft survived. 25 OTU, who pitched in at least 30 Wellingtons, also lost one machine and so did 26 OTU out of Wing; the two bombers being Wellington IC, DV434 and Wellington IC, HX375 respectively.

27 OTU at Lichfield mustered 20 Wellington ICs for the attack. Several aircrew who had flown on the Cologne raid relived the experience again but on this occasion the raid was less eventful. Sgt H Richardson and his crew probably had the closest encounter with the enemy that night. Whilst over The Hague, the bomber was held in several searchlights at 8,000ft. Richardson dived down to 200ft to escape the lights and flew north out to sea while the front and rear gunners fired at the searchlights. The machine gun fire attracted the attention of an enemy night fighter which closed in on the tail of the Wellington. The rear gunner had just enough time to fire a short burst of fire at the fighter when the Wellington was hit by light anti-aircraft fire from a ship. Part of the geodetic structure of the bomber was damaged, an oil pipe was ruptured and the navigator's table and chair were destroyed by the shell as it passed through the aircraft. Luckily, the navigator was up front with the

pilot at the time. The offending oil pipe was repaired with chewing gum and the bomber, like all of its colleagues, returned home to Lichfield.

Also worthy of mention are the smaller units which contributed to this operation in order to give, or at least try to give, Harris his magic number again. 1429 Flight managed to detail three of its Wellingtons which had also flown on the Cologne operation and had remained at Feltwell. All came home safely and so did the one and only contribution from Flying Training Command which was 1 AAS, Wellington IC, P9295 again flown by Fg Off Chown and crew. The experience gained by this crew would have proved invaluable once they returned to the home of 1 AAS at Manby to continue their training role. As mentioned earlier, aircraft were again contributed by several Target Towing and Gunnery Flights including No.1481 from Binbrook, 1483 at Newmarket and possibly 1484 from Driffield. 1502 BATF also at Driffield also contributed five Whitley Vs. 3 Group's 1651 CU may have contributed at least half a dozen Stirlings and Leonard Cheshire's 1652 CU, as mentioned earlier, contributed a similar number of Halifax IIs.

The final stages

With fires of varying sizes continuing to appear over a wide area, the raid began to subside with the arrival of those crews who took off late, mainly because of last-minute technical issues. One of those was Flt Sgt Rochford and crew in their 10 Squadron Halifax II, W7696 'H' which was destined to be the last aircraft to drop its bombs at 0227hrs from 13,000ft. While many crews had described the defences as weak and apparently disorganised, Rochford described the flak as 'intense and accurate and searchlights were active in large numbers,' which is testament to the determination and organisation of the defenders. Another Halifax, Mk II, W1058 'S' flown by Plt Off Drake and crew, also from 10 Squadron, took off a mere eight minutes after Rochford but were forced to turn back as they could not make up the time needed to reach the primary target. Not to be denied their chance to contribute something to the war effort, Drake attacked a flak ship off the Dutch coast and then landed back at Leeming at 0437hrs satisfied that he had at least played some part in this huge operation.

The outcome

As we can already gather from the snippets of pilot reports mentioned earlier, there was much doubt from many crews as to whether they were over the target or not thanks to haze and cloud cover. The former was a common problem in the Ruhr. Essen was a particularly difficult target to locate and therefore it had escaped serious bombing many times before. Despite the number of aircraft despatched and the fact that many claimed to have bombed the primary target of the Krupps Works, no damage was reported from the giant weapon-producing company. Even Essen authorities only reported 15 people killed and a further 91 injured. A mere eleven houses were destroyed and 184 damaged in the southern half of the city and a POW work camp was also hit and razed to the ground. Many in Essen that night actually thought the main thrust was aimed elsewhere, which is more than possible considering that at least 14 other towns in the area reported bombs falling. Of this group, Oberhausen suffered the most, reporting 83 killed, followed by Duisburg with 52 killed and Mülheim with 15 killed. Bombs also fell on Bochum, Cologne, Gelsenkirchen, Gramenhage, Hafen III, Hamborn, Holton, Neuss, Steebe, Vorhafen and Wesel. Disregarding those airfields attacked by 2 and 11 Groups, both Gelden and Katwljk Anzel airfields were also bombed.

Good quality aerial reconnaissance images were provided by a pair of 105 Squadron Mosquito IVs, the first of them, W4071 with Ft Lt Parry at the controls took off from Horsham St Faith at 0610hrs on June 2 for a high-level bombing and photographic sortie. Parry and his navigator, Plt Off Robson, bombed and photographed Essen from 19,000ft and were safely back on the ground at 0815hrs. At that same moment a second aircraft, Mosquito IV, W4065 crewed by Sgts Rowland and Carreck flew the exact same sortie and two hours, ten minutes later were also back down at Horsham St Faith. A third aircraft was despatched by 105 Squadron in the shape of W4069 crewed by Plt Offs Paget and Addinsell at 1115hrs to bomb and photograph Cologne which would have been most likely still burning but beginning to reveal the true extent of the damaged caused on May 30/31, in stark contrast to Essen. Only minutes after Robson had taxied into his dispersal at Horsham St Faith, the magazines containing many feet of precious film would have been rapidly transported to the Photographic Section and processed in no time at all. Only once the film had been printed and despatched to High Wycombe would the dawning realisation that Essen had been virtually untouched began to hit home although, in typical RAF 'the glass is half full' mentality, some success was gleaned from the amount of damage caused to Oberhausen, Duisburg and Mülheim.

An RAF loss rate of 3.2% was soon forgotten by the senior commanders which equated to 37 bombers lost or involved in accidents as a result of the operation. 149 airmen had been killed, 46 were in captivity while three managed to evade it.

Essen Losses

RAF Losses

7 Sqn	Stirling I, N3750 'MG-D'; Lost off Dutch coast – 7 POW
10 OTU	Whitley V, Z6581 'P'; Shot down by night fighter, nr Breedenbroek – 5+
10 Sqn	Halifax II, L9623 'ZA-O'; Ditched off Dutch coast – 1+
	Halifax II, W1098 'ZA-W'; Crashed at Oeding – 6+ 1 POW
11 OTU	Wellington IC, DV767 'UP-J'; FTR – 4+ 1 POW
12 OTU	Wellington IC, X3203; Hit by flak over target – 1+ 4 POW
13 Sqn	Blenheim IV, Z6186 'E'; FTR – 3+
16 OTU	Wellington IC, DV763 'XG-H2'; Crashed at Perk – 2+ 2 POW 1 EVD
18 OTU	Wellington IC, HF891 'N'; 5+
20 OTU	Wellington IC, X9975; Lost off Dutch coast – 6+
21 OTU	Wellington IC, W5618 'W'; FTR – 5+ 1 POW
23 OTU	Wellington IC, R1266 'G2'; Crashed at Kerkdriel – 5+
	Wellington IC, Z8867 'L'; FTR – 5+
25 OTU	Wellington IC, DV434 'F2'; Crashed at Horst – 1+ 5 POW
26 OTU	Wellington IC, HX375 'X'; FTR – 5+
49 Sqn	Manchester I, R5794; Shot down by night fighter, Voorheide – 5+ 2 POW
57 Sqn	Wellington IC, DV816; FTR – 5 POW
61 Sqn	Lancaster I, R5544; Crashed nr Düsseldorf – 6+ 1 POW
76 Sqn	Halifax II, W1064 'MP-J'; Shot down by night fighter, nr Bossut – 2+ 2 POW 2 EVD
78 Sqn	Halifax II, R9364; Hit by flak off Dutch coast – 4+ 2 POW
	Halifax II, W1142 'EY-F'; Crashed off Hellevoetsluis – 6+, 1 POW
	Halifax II, W7698; Collided with night fighter, crashed Winterswijk – 3+ 3 POW
83 Sqn	Lancaster I, R5564 'OL-P'; Lost over the sea – 7+
97 Sqn	Lancaster I, R5571 'OF-A'; FTR – 7+
102 Sqn	Halifax II, R9529 'DY-H'; Crashed nr Düsseldorf – 6+
106 Sqn	Lancaster I, R5844; FTR – 7+
114 Sqn	Blenheim IV, R3620 'RT-A'; FTR – 3+
	Blenheim IV, V6337 'RT-D'; Hit by flak, crashed in the Channel – 3+
115 Sqn	Wellington III, X3721 'KO-F'; LWT – 5+
142 Sqn	Wellington IV, Z1410 'QT-Z'; Crashed at Thoresby Bridge – 5+ 1 inj
218 Sqn	Stirling I, N3753 'HA-U'; Crash landed at Marham – All safe
305 Sqn	Wellington II, Z8583 'SM-Z'; Crashed nr Billingford – 6+
405 Sqn	Halifax II, W7713 'LQ-T'; Crashed nr Krefeld – 7+

408 Sqn	Hampden I, AT191 'EQ-A'; Shot down by a night fighter, Ijsselmeer – 4+
460 Sqn	Wellington IV, Z1311 'UV-Z'; FTR – 6+
	Wellington IV, Z1344 'UV-W'; Crashed River Schelde – 2+ 3 POW 1 inj
1652 CU	Halifax II, R9372 'GV-K'; Shot down nr Dutch coast – 6 POW

Operation Millennium II

Bremen (June 25/26)

'Arabian Nights'

Following the disappointing raid on Essen, the Thousand Bomber Force was disbanded. The OTUs returned to their normal training duties while Bomber Command's squadrons continued, on average, 200-strong raids into Germany. It was time to keep the pressure up but even those close to Harris were surprised when he called for another raid on Essen on June 2/3, 5/6 and again on 16/17 before this massive force of bombers was drawn together again for a third raid in attempt to shake Germany to core. Raids were also carried out against Bremen and Emden but maintaining this level of operations had cost Bomber Command a disturbing 126 aircraft, a figure Harris could ill afford to lose if he was to carry out a third 'Thousand Plan'.

Completely convinced that his thousand-strong method of attack was the way forward, Harris once again proposed to Portal that another such raid was needed and at regular intervals during the full moon period. Again, Churchill and Portal were keen on the idea; the PM jokingly called these attacks 'Arabian Nights'. The subject of Coastal Command must have been on the agenda again as, on June 15, Churchill penned the following to the First Lord and First Sea Lord; 'It will be necessary to repeat the 1,000 operation in the June moon. On the coming occasions it will be necessary that Coastal Command should participate, and I must ask, definitely ask, for compliance with this request.'

The following day, First Sea Lord, Sir Dudley Pound responded during a Chiefs of Staff meeting stating that he had no intention '...to stop the bombing of Germany but that he was anxious that priority should be given to the improvement of our position at sea, which, in his opinion, was more vital and of greater urgency, particularly since the bombing of Germany was a long term project.' Regardless, The Admiralty yielded and offered up over 100 aircraft made up of Wellingtons and Hudsons plus a few Beaufighters in support. As a result, Harris was able to not only make use of the most diverse range of aircraft ever fielded against Germany during one operation, but also the largest number – 1,067. It would be known as Operation *Millennium II*, which begs the question to why the raid on Essen was not known by that name?

The plan

The overall plan for the main force was little different from that practised for Cologne and Essen, other than the fact that the bombing window had been reduced to 65 minutes. There were four primary targets allocated to the main force; 5 Group, which would field 142 aircraft, was tasked with attacking the Focke-Wulf Flugzeugbau AG factory. 20 Blenheims, normally accustomed to flying intruder operations were given the A.G. Weser shipyard (a specific yard within Deschimag [*Deutsche Schiff- und Maschinen Aktiengesellshaft*] complex) to bomb. All 102 of the Coastal Command aircraft taking part, made up of 20 Wellingtons and 82 Hudsons, were briefed to attack the Deschimag shipyards, while the remainder of the main force had the easier task of performing a general area attack upon Bremen and its shipyards. It is worth noting that by giving Coastal Command this target, Bomber Command could use the argument that Deschimag was one of the main production hubs for U-boats and that this would be an extension of the anti-U-boat campaign. With Churchill stepping in, The Admiralty was forced to comply but there was a serious argument against Coastal Command not taking part, including the fact that over 18,000tons of bombs had been dropped on U-boat factories and bases up to 1943 and not one U-boat had been damaged or put out of action. In contrast, there had been great success scored at sea which literally involved a single 25lb rocket or a 250lb depth charge not only resulting in the loss of the U-boat but also of an expensive highly trained crew. Politics aside, the Coastal Command crews were very excited to take part in such a huge operation.

One again, a lead 'marker force' would be employed equipped with *GEE*, dropping flares ahead of the main force. The weather report was encouraging as well; Bremen was free of cloud and, as such, hopes were high that this raid would strike the same blow as Cologne; the operation to Essen having been already pushed to back of the senior commanders' minds.

The intruders field a bigger force

Compared to the previous two 'Thousand Plan' raids, the intruder force employed for Bremen was much larger, with twelve units involved provided by 2 and 11 Groups, Army Co-Operation Command and Coastal Command. The latter was the Beaufighter-equipped 235 Squadron which was more used to flying anti-submarine operations.

More accustomed to flying post-raid assessment sorties, the operation began with 105 Squadron at Horsham St Faith at 2129hrs when Flt Lt Parry and Plt Off Robson took off in Mosquito IV, W4070. 21 minutes later, they were followed by Plt Off Costello-Brown and W/O Broom in W4066; both crews were briefed to attack the airfield at Schleswig/Jagel, over 60 miles north of Hamburg. Parry was unable to locate the airfield while Costello-Brown claimed to have dropped his bombs along the main runway. One minute after Parry took-off, the first of two aircraft contributed by 139 Squadron also took off from Oulton. 139 Squadron had only reformed at Horsham St Faith on June 8 and, for this operation, were borrowing aircraft from 105 Squadron. First away for 139 Squadron was Fg Off (Acting Sqn Ldr) J E Houlston and Flt Sgt J Armitage in Mosquito IV, DK296 followed by Flt Lt R B Bagguley and Fg Off A K Hayden at 2135hrs in W4072. Both crews were tasked with bombing the airfield at Stade, Houlston attacking at low level (100ft) as enemy aircraft were taking off. Bagguley failed to find Stade and instead bombed the town of Dorum north of Bremerhaven from an eye-watering 50ft. All four Mosquitoes returned safely, although Bagguley, whose flaps had been torn off when he selected them instead of the bomb bay doors, was forced to land fast and over-ran the runway, extensively damaging the aircraft.

Next up was another newcomer to night intruder operations, namely 226 Squadron under the command of Wg Cdr W E Surplice DFC equipped with the Boston III, operating out of Swanton Morley. The plan was for one 'vic' of three aircraft, led by Wg Cdr Surplice, to attack Jever airfield and a second 'vic' led by Sqn Ldr J F Castle to bomb Ardorf (Wittmund) airfield, the home of 2./NJG3, both at low level. All six Bostons departed Swanton Morley between 2142 and 2151hrs and remained together until the formation reached the Frisian Island of Baltrum, at which point the aircraft split into two 'vics'. Ardorf was attacked first at 2320hrs by Sqn Ldr Castle at the controls of Boston III, W8371 'F', accompanied by Flt Lt A B Wheeler and crew in AL741 'V' and Plt Off D T Smith and crew in AL750 'Z'. Between the three aircraft, five 500lb MC bombs with a time delay of eleven seconds, three 500lb GP with a 30 minute delay and four SBCs with a mixture of 4lb IBs and 9lb Anti-Tank bombs were scattered across the airfield. At least one 500lb bomb was seen to explode in the north-eastern corner of the runway while

226 Squadron Douglas Boston III, AL750 'Z' from an unusual angle. The bomber was part of the intruder force assigned to attack Jever airfield for Millennium II and was flown by Plt Off D T Smith.

A Boston III of 107 Squadron; a unit which was tasked with attacking the night fighter airfields at Leeuwarden and Bergen/Alkmaar.

other bombs fell near a hangar on the northern side of the airfield and across a southern dispersal. Various gun posts across the airfield were machine gunned, not to mention several *en route* to the target including Baltrum Island and also several Nissen-type huts were fired upon on Langeoog Island before the trio headed for home.

Meanwhile, Surplice began his attack on Jever at 2323hrs but at this point was only accompanied by Plt Off G F Henning and crew in AL710 'R' as Sqn Ldr G R Magill at the controls of AL679 'Y' was forced to break formation after being held by several searchlights. Over Jever, Surplice attacked from 100ft and Henning from 300ft, dropping an assortment of bombs similar to those dropped by the Castle-led 'vic'. Magill opted for a secondary target near a railway line within a wood not far from the airfield. Both attacks were received with a range of multi-calibre defences but all six escaped without any damage which was partly credited to poor visibility of less than one mile under 8/10ths cloud which began 2,000ft above the raiders. This was an early indication that the weather was not going to be as clear as expected over the target area.

614 Squadron, which had re-located from Macmerry, East Lothian to West Raynham on June 24 had eleven serviceable aircraft available for this operation. It would have been a round dozen but the undercarriage of Blenheim IV, V5457

collapsed at Macmerry as the aircraft taxied for take-off. The first of eleven aircraft to take-off from West Raynham was Flt Lt H G Munro in Z6104 at 2200hrs, one of three machines briefed to attack Ardorf airfield. Frustratingly for Munro, the mid-upper turret went unserviceable and 40 minutes later the Blenheim was back on the ground at West Raynham and out of the raid. Of the rest of the formation, five were briefed to attack Leeuwarden and three more to Vechta. Of the Leeuwarden raid, three Blenheims successfully bombed the airfield, another failed to find the target and Plt Off D Smyth and crew in R3758 also failed to find the airfield but bombed a railway junction near Leeuwarden instead. Of the remaining two crews allocated Ardorf as a target, one failed to locate it while Plt Off R L W Baelz and crew in N3536 did find the airfield and accurately bombed it. This left the three crews sent to Vechta, which all managed to bomb the airfield.

107 Squadron, under the command of Wg Cdr L Lynn, stationed at Great Massingham and another member of 2 Group was re-equipped from the Blenheim IV to the Boston III in February 1942. Since then it had flown 26 operations, all of them in daylight; Bremen would be the unit's first night intruder operation. The first of nine aircraft was led away from Great Massingham at 2207hrs by Sqn Ldr P R Barr and crew in Boston III, Z2286. The brief was for six aircraft to attack the airfield at Leeuwarden and three to bomb Bergen/Alkmaar airfield, all with a mixture of 500lb bombs with eleven second and 30-minute delays, 40lb A/T and IBs.

Led by Wg Cdr Lynn, the Leeuwarden group approached the Dutch coast at low level in three sections of two aircraft but the plan began to unravel thanks to the weather. 10/10ths cloud at about 2,000ft forced the formation to split up and find the airfield independently which was some task. Both Lynn and Plt Off J A Allen's crews failed to find Leeuwarden and found themselves spending more time avoiding flak and searchlights. As a result they returned to Great Massingham with full bomb loads. Two more crews also returned back to Norfolk without finding Leeuwarden which left just Sqn Ldr Barr and crew and Flt Lt A F Carlisle and crew in AL702. Both Bostons approached Leeuwarden a mere 100ft above the ground; Barr, leading, dropped his bombs across a dispersal area. Carlisle then followed but, just as he was about to drop his bombs, the delayed blast from one that Barr had just dropped exploded under AL702. Carlisle momentarily lost control as the blast ripped through the aircraft punching a large hole in the tailplane and shaking the mid-upper machine guns from their mounts to the horror of air gunner Sgt G Murray who then watched them slip overboard! Presumably, Carlisle managed to deliver his bombs and then limped back home.

Under similar weather conditions, the three aircraft briefed to attack Bergen/Alkmaar were forced to split up. Sqn Ldr Forsyth and crew, who led the formation, failed to find the airfield but Flt Lt R J McLachlan at the controls of AL747 and Plt Off T J Rushton flying AL266 didn't. McLachlan, determined not to be taken down by local defences, made his run at 75ft across the southwestern corner of the airfield at 2312hrs and claimed to hit five to six parked enemy aircraft. Two minutes later, Rushton made his run at 100ft, shooting up the hangars with the Boston's front guns as he went. Bombs were dropped across the middle of airfield, at which point the aircraft was caught in a pair of searchlights which were promptly shot out. As a souvenir of his attack, the airfield defences did manage to shoot off the top of the Boston's rudder but Rushton was still able to get it back home to Great Massingham.

The Boston III-equipped 88 Squadron had been involved in the both the Cologne and Essen operations, but only in an ASR capacity in the search for downed crews in the North Sea. They were well-used to operating over the Continent on hairy low-level daylight raids but were strangers to night intruder operations and the squadron only began night flying practice late in May 1942. For the Bremen operation, 88 Squadron contributed nine aircraft which were led away from Attlebridge at 2225hrs by Flt Lt Phillips and crew in Boston III, Z2211. The nine aircraft were allocated three Dutch airfield targets, namely Gilze-Rijen, Haamstede and Valkenberg. The three aircraft briefed to attack Gilze-Rijen, led by Sqn Ldr England and crew in Z2216, were the least successful. All three Boston IIIs failed to find the airfield and all jettisoned their bombs into the sea off the Dutch coast. The next three Bostons, led by Plt Off Adams and crew in Z2260, achieved some success although Adams found himself making landfall five miles north of his intended track which ruined his bomb run while Flt Sgt Attenborough in Z2236 and Sgt Savage in Z2292 had time to correct their course in time to attack Haamstede located at the western edge of Schouwen Island. Attenborough dropped his bombs from 150ft, closely followed by Savage from the same height. Attenborough sharply turned his Boston around onto a reciprocal heading to see what damage had been caused and two lines of burning incendiaries were seen across the middle of the airfield with some more fires in the north western corner before the Bostons made their escape across the North Sea. Finally, it was down to Flt Lt Phillips to lead Sgt Hughes in AL690 and Sgt Simkins and crew in AL721 to attack Valkenberg airfield northeast of The Hague and again close to the coast. Phillips planted his bombs on the northern side of the airfield from 300ft while Sgt Hughes swooped down to 200ft dropping his bombs on the intersection between the main runway and western perimeter track. Sgt Simkins followed in at 150ft dropping his bombs on hangars and a dispersal area on the northern side of the airfield before all three banked hard to port and away for home across the open sea.

114 Squadron were no strangers to night intruder operations but, on this occasion they would also be taking part in the main raid. Initially, the squadron had

No strangers to low-level daylight operations over the Continent, the Bostons of 88 Squadron were allocated the airfields at Gilze-Rijen, Haamstede and Valkenberg for Millennium II.

15 aircraft and crew on standby for operations during June 25, but by that evening this had been reduced to 13 of which nine were detailed to attack Bremen, two to attack Vechta and another pair to Leeuwarden. Of the intruders, the first aircraft away from West Raynham was Sgt Parsons and crew Blenheim IV, Z6161 'Z', who, along with Plt Off Steele and crew in V5456 'V', were tasked to attack Vechta. Parsons was presented with a fully lit Vechta and, from 3,000ft at 0057hrs, dropped his bombs in the middle of the airfield and, even after his attack, the perimeter lights remained burning bright. Despite the briefing, Plt Off Steele attacked Ardorf, over 60 miles north of Vechta, from 2,700ft at 0125hrs, witnessing one large explosion and several smaller ones, possibly across the runways and hangars. Of the other two intruders tasked to attack Leeuwarden, Plt Off Thorburn on R3678 'A' left West Raynham at 2245hrs and at 0035hrs was over the airfield at 2,000ft dropping his bombs. Plt Off Owen and crew in Z7319 'P' were also due to attack Leeuwarden but, owing to bad visibility could not find the target and instead jettisoned their bombs into the sea where they were greeted with some fire from several flak ships

operating off the Dutch coast. The remainder of 114 Squadron, led by Wg Cdr Pollard and crew in V6262 'G', were tasked to attack Bremen and this force of nine aircraft began taking off from 2330hrs, all of them destined for a long sortie.

The first of two contributions from Coastal Command to the intruder part of this huge operation was a quartet of Beaufighter ICs supplied by 236 Squadron at Wattisham. The four aircraft were briefed to patrol the airfields at Schleswig/Jagel and Stade, although each Beaufighter would carry a pair of 250lb bombs. First aircraft away was X8086 'D' crewed by Flt Sgt A L Bonnett and Sgt Burden who at 2233hrs set course for Stade and once there would remain patrolling the area until relieved by Plt Off R Sherwood and Plt Off Freshwater in X8036 'S' who took off from Wattisham at 2314hrs. Whilst over Stade, Bonnett and Burden had a rough time, having been coned by searchlights at least three times which took some very violent evasive action to release their grip. Once relieved by Sherwood, Bonnet was forced to divert to Horsham St Faith with near empty tanks, most likely because of those manoeuvres over Stade. Meanwhile, Plt Off L C Lee and Flt Sgt Taylor in X7939 'B', had an equally uncomfortable time over Schleswig/Jagel thanks to very intensive and accurate flak and were lucky to get away safely before they were relieved. Plt Off H C Bateman and Sgt Robertson in T5131 'B' experienced the same level of accuracy of flak over Schleswig/Jagel but again got away without any damage and returned safely back to Wattisham.

By the time the first of nine Bostons, contributed again by 418 Squadron, took off out of Bradwell Bay at 2300hrs, a number of the main force were gaining altitude over England and setting course for Bremen. 418 Squadron's night would be highly successful; four aircraft were briefed to attack Gilze-Rijen, three to Deelen and a pair, including the aircraft of Wg Cdr A E Saunders, would patrol the Deelen area. The attack on Gilze-Rijen began at 0027hrs and, by the time the last of four Bostons had completed the raid, all 16 500lb bombs delivered had struck the runways and taxiways. Similar success was achieved at Deelen which was attacked at 0030hrs, it was all over in ten minutes and again explosions were observed on, or very near, the runways. All aircraft, including the two patrolling over Deelen, returned safely back to Bradwell Bay.

The second contribution from Coastal Command for intruder duties was 235 Squadron, another Beaufighter unit, which had moved south from Sumburgh to Docking on May 31, 1942. The six crews were briefed in similar fashion to the 235 Squadron crews although rather than patrolling Schleswig/Jagel and Stade airfields, they were ordered to attack them. Led away from Docking at 2306hrs by Flt M G Birt and Sgt G P Marsden, 235 Squadron's operation did not go well and, of the six Beaufighters, only one found their target. This was the crew of Beaufighter 'Q', Sgt A Norris and Sgt J D Walters, who located Schleswig/Jagel and successfully dropped a pair of 250lb bombs with three second delays onto the target.

The first of 15 crews of 18 Squadron joined the intruder fray at 2312hrs when Plt Off A W Eller and crew in Blenheim IV, V6317 took off from Wattisham. Of this batch of aircraft, four were detailed to attack Venlo, five to Twente, three to St Trond and finally four Blenheims to Bremen. Sqn Ldr H Malcolm led the four Blenheims briefed to attack Venlo with some success. Malcolm led a faultless attack against the airfield and all four machines dropped their loads of two 250lb bombs and 16 x 40lb IBs across the Venlo with little opposition. Twente proved to be a more challenging target as several decoys in the region were proving to be an effective distraction. However, four of the five Blenheims managed to bomb the primary target of Twente while Plt Off W Booth and crew in Blenheim IV, V6424 bombed Leeuwarden instead. Of the Twente group, Sgt Gibson and crew in V6971 were intercepted by an unknown enemy aircraft but managed to successfully evade it and fly safely home. The final intruder group allocated St Trond were the least successful and only Plt Off L Rule and crew in T2431 found the primary target and bombed it. Plt Off E Holloway and crew in V6395 failed to find St Trond and returned with their bombs while Plt Off P Lowther and crew in Z5879 were very lucky to make it back at all. The Blenheim was subjected to no less than ten attacks by enemy fighters all of which were shaken off and the rear gunner Sgt Drury claimed one of them destroyed. As a result of this over-attention, Lowther had a good excuse for not finding St Trond and he also returned back to Wattisham with a full bomb load.

Nine Blenheims from 13 Squadron were detailed for operations this night; five would attack Bremen while three were allocated St Trond and a single machine was despatched to Venlo. The first of the intruders, Blenheim IV, N3545 flown by Flt Lt Stathers took off from Wattisham at 2330hrs. Loaded with a mixture of 250lb GP Instantaneous, 250lb GP bombs with a 30 minute delay and 40lb Anti-Personal bombs, the attack did not go well and of those allocated St Trond, none found the target. Stathers was forced to bomb Liege airfield instead while Plt Off Woodland and crew in Z5895 attacked Brussels airfield. The third aircraft, Z6084 with Plt Off P G Frith at the controls was brought down by a night fighter piloted by Oblt Eckart-Wilhelm von Bonin of 6./NJG1. The Blenheim crashed near Houwaart, eight miles northeast of Leuven with the loss of all three aircrew. Unfortunately, the lone wolf operation to Venlo by Fg Off P H Looker and crew in T2254 was equally unsuccessful and they also fell to the guns of a night fighter with the loss of all on board.

The final stage of the intruder 'bombing' element of this operation began at 2340hrs when Sqn Ldr Starr and his 23 Squadron crew lifted their Havoc I from Manston's runway bound for Eindhoven. Six Havocs were detailed to attack

Eindhoven, a further three Bostons, operating from Ford would attack Juvincourt and another pair of Bostons were briefed to patrol the Juvincourt area. All six Havoc crews scored hits against Eindhoven airfield, the majority of them witnessing the effects of their attack before all turned safely for home. All three Boston crews also had successful raids against Juvincourt and Plt Off F P Coventry and crew achieved the bonus of attacking three trains, one of which blew up, a second ground to a halt while the third continued on its way. Plt Off G L Shemilt and crew also machine gunned a train near Laon.

Sqn Ldr James A F MacLachlan, DSO, DFC the commanding officer of 1 Squadron. MacLachlan lost the lower part of his left leg during combat in Malta but this did not deter him from returning to the cockpit.

The last intruders to take part in the Bremen operation were the Hurricane IICs of 1 Squadron operating out of Manston. The first of five Hurricanes flown by Sqn Ldr J A F MacLachlan, DSO, DFC took off from Manston at 0058hrs and the last was away by 0015hrs. Briefed to patrol Gilze-Rijen, MacLachlan was unable to find the airfield due to his map being blown 'overboard' *en route*. Czech Flt Lt K Kuttelwascher DFC was also briefed to patrol Gilze-Rijen but he, along with MacLachlan, would go home empty-handed that night. Sgt G S M Pearson had a more interesting patrol witnessing at least one bomber falling in flames and another burning on the ground not to mention a close encounter with a Bf 110 which he was unable to turn into an attack thanks to Luftwaffe flak being fired at the enemy night fighter! New Zealander, Plt Off D P Perrin, was destined to score a first for 1 Squadron when he flew as far west as Dusseldorf, becoming the first 1 Squadron intruder to penetrate Germany, such was the good range of the Hurricane IIC. Sgt Campbell also witnessed at least two burning aircraft on the ground in the Eindhoven area and tried to chase an enemy night fighter but failed to catch it. On his return, he strafed a couple of trains between Antwerp and Turnhout, both of which blew up. That turned out to be only the success for 1 Squadron that night. Unfortunately, WO G Scott, RCAF in HL789, who was also meant to patrol Gilze-Rijen, failed to return and was killed.

While the cumulative effect of this large intruder operation was not known at the time, regardless of success, these crews were providing a worthwhile distraction to the Luftwaffe defences who would rather have been chasing down bombers high above instead of defending the night fighter airfields.

The main force rises

Just like 105 Squadron, which had begun the proceedings over an hour earlier, 35 Squadron was destined to become one of the founding units of the Pathfinder Force. It was therefore appropriate that this experienced bomber squadron led the way for this latest 'Thousand Plan' operation. 18 Halifax IIs were detailed for this operation and the first away was W1006 'I' piloted by Sgt McDonald at 2235hrs. Unfortunately, three Halifaxes had to turn back with mechanical problems, such as an unserviceable rear turret, port inner engine and starboard engine; the latter forcing McDonald and crew to turn back and jettison their bombs into the sea. Of the remaining 15 aircraft, 14 are known to have bombed Bremen while Fg Off H G B Mays and crew in Halifax II, W1105 'N' failed to return. Most likely *en route*, and a mere 20 miles short of the target, the bomber was hit by flak at 14,000ft over Oldenburg and crashed nearby; two of the seven crew survived to become POWs.

Another future Pathfinder unit was 156 Squadron who, like 35 Squadron, were briefed to drop flares on the target. 20 crews were detailed to take part, including one borrowed from the BATF at Wyton. The first away from Alconbury was Wellington III, X3728, flown by Flt Lt Gilmour and crew, at 2245hrs. The inevitable batch of early returners began to suffer a variety of unforeseen problems including Sgt W P Thompson and crew in BJ594 with electrical failure. At 0016hrs at 8,000ft, Thompson turned the bomber back towards Alconbury whilst over Southwold and prepared his crew for an emergency landing. With no option of jettisoning the bomb load other than steering north to The Wash, it would be no easy task to put this Wellington down safely and, on arrival at Alconbury Thompson had already been forced to overshoot twice before attempting a third and final landing. It did not go well; the bomber hit the ground hard and struck a concrete pillbox which tore the rear fuselage away, along with the rear gunner, Sgt H F Young. All crew who were forward escaped injury but the 33 year old Londoner trapped in his turret was fatally injured and died a few minutes later.

Meanwhile, the first of the remaining 156 Squadron Wellingtons had reached the target although they had already been overtaken by a number of other squadrons all flying the same route but at different speeds and slightly different heights. This was Sgt Longhurst and crew in Z1613 who dropped 450 x 4lb IBs and 32 x 30lb IBs on Bremen at 0125hrs from 14,000ft on a T.R. fix. *En route* Longhurst recorded that they had seen what they believed to be a twin-engine enemy aircraft going down in flames over Polder and three more aircraft, most likely British, also tumbling earthbound over the target. A number of 156 Squadron Wellingtons also had scrapes with night fighters but all were shaken off thanks to good crew discipline and co-operation.

The marking had been pretty accurate so far although this did not stop towns around Bremen also receiving some unwanted attention. The first of 10 Squadron's 15 Halifax IIs (which again also included machines from 10CF), flown by Flt Sgt Allen and crew, was away from Leeming at 2247hrs and the first to attack Bremen was W1058 'S' flown by Plt Off Drake at 0122hrs. Nine crews claimed to have bombed the primary target in a display of concentrated bombing which took just ten minutes to carry out before they all turned for home. Over Bremen, the flak was described by crews as something between moderate and intense and accurate. Flt Sgt Allen's sortie was shorter than planned thanks to the pilot's hatch blowing off while he was changing seats for some unknown reason, resulting in bombs being jettisoned into the sea and a return to Leeming long before his colleagues had reached Bremen. Sgt Wyatt and crew in Halifax II, W7697 'R' also had a shorter than planned trip thanks to a failed artificial horizon and altimeter forcing another early return. Another unserviceability aboard R9495 'M' flown by Flt Sgt Clarke and crew was in the shape of a faulty air speed indicator resulting in the town of Lathan being bombed rather than Bremen. Wilhelmshaven, which would receive many bombs during the operation, was attacked by Plt Off Kenny and Crew in R9177 'V' at 0132hrs and again by Sgt Gibbons and crew in W1028 'O' at 0218hrs. Oldenburg, just over 20 miles short of Bremen, would also be hit several times before the night was over including the bomb load of W1003 'K' flown by Flt Sgt Saunders at 0209hrs. It was a mixed result for 10 Squadron, but all would return home to Yorkshire safe.

Another 4 Group unit, 76 Squadron, which would serve as part of 'marker force' for this operation, was led away from Middleton St George by Sqn Ldr Iveson and crew in Halifax II, W7672 'E' at 2251hrs. 76 Squadron managed to field 14 aircraft for the latest 'Thousand Plan' although three of this number were contributed by 76CF. 15 crews were actually briefed but the aircraft allocated to Plt Off Dobmen and crew, R9378 (a 76CF aircraft), caught fire after several IBs ignited after falling from the bomb bay because of an electrical fault. Eight crews were selected as 'markers'; these Halifaxes departed Middleton St George first with orders to attack Bremen on a T.R fix at an average height of 13,000ft between 0122 and 0139hrs. Not all would make it but one aircraft that did was Halifax II, W7702 'L', flown by Flt Lt Renaut and crew who were presented with a target covered by 8/10ths to 10/10ths cloud between 3,000 and 5,000ft. Determined to see his marker task through, Renaut descended to a dangerous 2,500ft and began his bomb run at a speed of 280mph. It was at this point that the Halifax was suddenly held in the grasp of three searchlights which blinded the bomb aimer. Renaut was still able to see the centre of Bremen and, on his command, the bomb aimer delivered their payload at 0139hrs. It was an agonising three minutes before Renaut managed to shake the searchlights off and, as soon as the bombs had been dropped, the mixture was turned to rich, the throttles were pushed wide open and the control column was pulled back to regain height as quickly as possible and reach the sanctuary of the cloud. The flak was intense at that altitude but light and although some hits were scored by the defences, Renaut and his crew got away with it. Only six of the markers claimed to have bombed the centre of Bremen and, of the six remaining Halifaxes due to follow behind, four of them managed to bomb from an average height of 14,000ft between 0151 and 0210hrs. The two markers that did not reach the target were Plt Off Raymond and crew W7655 'O' who were forced to turn back early because of a glycol leak in the port outer followed by overheating of the port inner engine. Flt Sgt Clack and crew in W7755 'A' had to jettison their bomb load 30 miles off the Dutch coast and then return to base because of an intercom and oxygen failure. For Sqn Ldr Calder and crew in Halifax II, R9387 'Z', their trip to Bremen was one that they were lucky to return from and it was not just the enemy who took umbrage to them. *En route* to the target, and with no sign of night fighters, the crew were shocked to suddenly come under fire whilst over the Dutch town of Hoorn. To their horror, they had actually been attacked by a nervous air gunner in a Wellington and his aim was good, because the starboard outer engine was put out of action. With little choice but to turn for home, Calder had just jettisoned the Halifax's bomb load when the bullets started flying again, this time from a night fighter which had crept up from below the bomber, 30 miles west northwest of Alkmaar. Calder managed to outmanoeuvre the night fighter but not before two of his crew were slightly injured and, instead of heading for Middleton, an emergency landing at Coltishall was successfully made instead. One 76 Squadron Halifax failed to return, this was W7747 with Sgt J E Meyer, RCAF, at the controls, supported by his all-sergeant crew; they were grimly lost without trace.

Coastal Command joins the fray

As we already know, The Admiralty had made the decision not to allow aircraft under its charge to take part in *Millennium* to Cologne on May 25. That same day, one Coastal Command unit, 24 Hudsons of 1 (Coastal) OTU, stationed at Silloth, had already re-located to its assigned forward operating base at Thornaby, under the control of 18 Group Coastal Command. For *Millennium II*, there would be no disappointment for the crews and another 24 Hudsons of various marks descended upon Thornaby again. Loaded with four 250lb bombs apiece, the aircraft were

304 Squadron, Wellington IC, DV441, possibly pictured at Dale just before Millennium II. The bomber was shot down by a night fighter into the North Sea; all six crew were killed. www.aircrewremembered.com

allocated a variety of coastal targets mainly in Holland, in an operation classed as a diversion rather than an intruder and unique amongst the 'Thousand Plan'.

Only one aircraft failed to return from this diversion operation. Hudson I, P5147, piloted by Sqn Ldr W D Hodgkinson DFC, an instructor and flight commander, was brought down by a night fighter near De Kooy. Only Hodgkinson and his observer, Fg Off V F Cave, managed to bail out while the two wireless operator/air gunners, Fg Off E H Tomlinson and Plt Off R E S Summers, were killed. Hodgkinson and Cave saw the war out as POWs, the former spending some of his internment in Stalag Luft 3 and later surviving the 'Long March' in 1945. Hodgkinson remained in the RAF after the war and, after reaching the rank of air vice marshal, did not retire until 1976.

The first of six Coastal Command squadrons to contribute to the 'Thousand Plan' were the Wellingtons of 304 Squadron. Having only recently moved from Tiree in the Inner Hebrides down to Dale in Pembrokeshire, the seven Wellingtons detailed for this operation would be flying from Docking. Loaded with six 500lb bombs apiece, the first aircraft away was Wellington IC, DV803, flown by Fg Off W Konarzewski and crew at 2250hrs. Sgt W Sicinski at the controls of DV836 was the first 304 Squadron crew to bomb Bremen through 10/10ths cloud from 6,000ft. However, Konarzewski was the first to drop his bombs at 0115hrs on Bremer-Vorde thanks to the attentions of a Bf 110 and flak. The Bf 110 loosed off a number of rounds at the Wellington, which was hit, but still managed to return back to Docking with little trouble or injury to the crew. Of the remainder, four are confirmed to have bombed Bremen and all describe bomb bursts and the glow of fires, even through the thick cloud.

Unfortunately, there was no news of Sgt H Kuc and his crew in DV441 which is believed to have been shot down by a night fighter into the North Sea with the loss of all six crew. Only the body of Fg Off M Dydzuil was recovered from the water; he was given an immediate military funeral and returned to the sea.

Under the control of 16 Group, Coastal Command from February 1940, the sleepy airfield at North Coates, south of Cleethorpes was still a few months away from reaching its true purpose during the Second World War when it would become the home of one of the RAF's many effective Strike Wings. Up to this time, a few Blenheim units had made the remote airfield their home but the arrival of two more units in preparation for *Millennium II* suddenly brought the place alive. 59 Squadron and its Hudson Vs, under the command of Wg Cdr G C C Bartlett, had been the resident unit at North Coates from January 1942. On June 23, the number of aircrew and groundcrew suddenly swelled with the arrival of eleven aircraft from Tiree in the shape of 224 Squadron, operating the Hudson III and V, with further aircraft arriving later the same day. The latter belonged to 206 Squadron who brought another dozen Hudsons all the way from Aldergrove but, on their arrival, were ordered to re-locate their aircraft to the small satellite airfield just four miles down the road, and ten minutes flying time, at Donna Nook where they would be prepared for the raid.

First away from North Coates was Wg Cdr Bartlett and crew in Hudson V, AM564 at 2300hrs. Rising away from North Coates main runway, which butted up to a flood bank, within seconds Bartlett was over the sea and setting course for Bremen. Ten minutes later the first of eleven aircraft from 224 Squadron also began taking off from North Coates; the first of them flown by Sqn Ldr A S Miryless and crew in Hudson V, AM757 'K'. Simultaneously, 206 Squadron began to rise from the tiny satellite at Donna Nook, led away by Sqn Ldr C N Crook and crew, which included the officer commanding, Wg Cdr H D Cooke, who had only taken over the unit on June 12, in AM762 'S'. The operation for 59 Squadron appears to have been an uneventful one; all twelve Hudsons claimed to have bombed the Deschimag shipyard as briefed but were also greeted by heavy cloud over the target so results could not be observed. Wg Cdr Bartlett circled Bremen for over 30 minutes in an effort to see the results of his squadron's work but saw very little. All of 59 Squadron's Hudsons returned safely, although Bartlett landed at Catfoss to refuel before reaching North Coates at 0700hrs.

For 224 Squadron, Sqn Ldr Miryless was the first to attack the target at 0148hrs with a pair of 250lb A/S and eight 100lb A/S bombs. The crew were lucky to have survived let alone drop their bombs as, only minutes earlier, a large fragment of an anti-aircraft shell had sliced its way through the nose without injury to anyone. Prior to reaching the target at 0053hrs, Fg Off D Sleep and crew in Hudson III, V9092 'A', were attacked by a pair of Bf 110s with cannon fire whilst flying at 8,000ft. Sleep

206 Squadron aircrew at Aldergrove on April 21, 1942. From the left, Sgts Joe Peet, Les Goodson, Ted Nelson and Flt Sgt Alan Marriot. Joe Peet was destined to bail out of his crippled Hudson to become a POW while the remainder returned home. The late Ted Nelson

took violent evasive action and managed to escape the night fighters by diving into a layer of cloud at 6,000ft. Having escaped being hit on this occasion, Sleep continued on to Bremen but, on sighting a single-engine fighter over Borkum at 8,000ft, he instantly dived down to cloud cover again, this time at 4,000ft where he then attracted the attention of the local defences. Determined to carry out his task, Sleep saw Bremen ahead, given away by a red glow seeping through the clouds. The clouds looked impenetrable initially, averaging 9/10ths and topping out at 9,000ft. However, a gap suddenly opened up and Sleep dropped a pair of 250lb

A/S and seven 100lb A/S bombs before making his escape and a less eventful return flight to North Coates. Flt Sgt G B Willerton and crew in Hudson V, AM779 'U' were also lucky to make it home when a heavy flak burst directly below them and exploded with such a force it blew a beam gun clean out of the aircraft.

It was 206 Squadron who were destined to take the brunt of the losses from this batch of Coastal Command Hudsons although nine of the twelve Hudsons involved claimed to have bombed Bremen while a tenth attacked Wilhelmshaven. The squadron found the task of singling out the Deschimag shipyard almost impossible because of the heavy cloud and instead bombed near to the fires which were already taking hold. Two aircraft failed to return; Sqn Ldr Crook's aircraft and AM606 'M' flown by Sgt K D Wright and crew; only two crew from the latter, Sgts J H Peet and J W Speed survived to become POWs.

One of the aircrew that took part in the 206 Squadron operation was wireless operator/air gunner, Sgt E 'Ted' H Nelson, who was part of Fg Off A E Bland's crew in Hudson V, AM722 'G'. He recalled the sortie vividly:

> 'On the 25th, with a thousand other aircraft, we flew out over the North Sea, heading for the German city of Bremen; it truly was an unbelievable sight. In every direction there were aircraft as far as the eye could see. Black shapes silhouetted against the night sky.
>
> The overall flight lasted six hours and thirty five minutes and was packed with incidents. One's first sight of flak and of anti-aircraft fire was quite exciting. It was all so colourful, so concentrated, yet we seemed to pass it by in the early stages. The closer we flew to Bremen the more intense it became until finally we reached our target.
>
> I will never, ever, forget my first sighting of a German city in flames, with super-bright searchlights weaving around and an aerial firework display produced by the exploding Ack Ack shells. The whole scene was hypnotic and it was only the calm voice of the pilot, Eric Bland, talking to the Navigator/Bomb Aimer on the bombing run that brought one back to reality and made me realise that this had nothing to do with Guy Fawkes. This was for real!
>
> One marvelled at the way so many aircraft could be concentrated in one area and yet not collide, and that the bursting shells did not seem to be hitting the aircraft. Guess we were so very fortunate as far too many shells did find their target. In fact, forty eight of the total force 'Failed to Return'. We stayed long enough to complete our bombing run and to see hundreds of explosions on the ground. Then our Skipper did the sensible thing and set course for England.

On return to Donna Nook, in the half light of pre-dawn, the North Sea looks very inhospitable and having spent quite a while avoiding hostile flak and night fighters we were not at all sure of our position and were running very low on fuel. In the Operations Room there was real concern as 25% of the squadron's planes had then 'Failed to Return', including the one containing our new commanding officer Wg Cdr Cooke.

Our Skipper fortunately sighted a smudge on the horizon, the east coast of Britain and with five pairs of eyes scanning the rapidly approaching land we were soon able to identify the area and raced to North Coates to find out that we had already been recorded as 'Missing', as it was recognised that by then we should have run out of fuel; in fact, the ground crew confirmed that there were only minutes of flying time remaining in the tanks.

The other two 'Missing' aircraft did 'Fail to Return', having been shot down over target. One of them contained my crew mate and best friend, Joe Peet, who spent the rest of the war in various German POW camps. After the war, at a 206 Squadron re-union, he told the story of how he 'fell out' of his Hudson over the burning city of Bremen and was fortunately captured before he could be lynched by some very, very angry survivors of our bombing.'

Also under the charge of 16 Group Coastal Command was the northwest Norfolk airfield of Bircham Newton and its satellite at nearby Docking. Bircham Newton was already a busy airfield with no less than five squadrons in residence, two of which, 320 (Netherlands) and 407 (Demon) Squadrons, would be taking part in *Millennium II*. The airfield became even busier on June 24 when the first of twelve Wellington ICs of 311(Czechoslovak) Squadron began to arrive from Talbenny in Pembrokeshire which would force 320 (Netherlands) Squadron, who could only muster four Hudson IIIs, to re-locate and operate from Docking.

23.6.42	2125	AM 822	P/Sgt	BIDDELL	PASSENGER		NORTH COATES TO DONNA NOOK	0.10	
							MILLENNIUM TWO		
25.6.42	2320	AM 722	P/O	BLAND	36 AG O=		MASS BOMBING RAID ON BREMEN	✱ 6.35
							TARGET BOMBED. 2 A/C LOST INCLUDING TOO LATE = 6000% NEW	
26.6.42	0815	AM 722	P/O	WOOSLEY	PASSENGER		NORTH COATES TO DONNA NOOK	0.10	
27.6.42		AM 722	P/O		PASSENGER		DONNA NOOK TO BIRCHAM NE		

The entry in Ted Nelson's logbook for 'Millennium Two' with reference to the two Hudsons lost; it was a sortie which lasted 6hrs 35mins. The late Ted Nelson

First away from Bircham Newton was the 311 Squadron Wellington IC, HF921 'N' of Fg Off Taibr and crew who took off at 2303hrs. All appeared to go smoothly until Sgt Zebulka opened the throttles of Z1090 'Q' at 2327hrs, only to hit a hut on the edge of airfield just moments before the bomber lifted into the air. The Wellington was seriously damaged but Zebulka kept his head and with no chance of jettisoning the bomb load, he put the aircraft down safely in Brancaster Bay, just seven miles north of the airfield without causing any injuries to his crew. Of the remainder, one Wellington had to abandon the operation through flap failure and another returned early with engine trouble, leaving just nine to bomb Bremen through thick cloud. It was not the best of operations for 311 Squadron and on his return Flt Lt Horejdi at the controls of Z1111 'N' hit the brakes a little too hard forcing the bomber onto its nose; an undignified evacuation of the Wellington followed but all were uninjured.

Over at Docking, the four 320 Squadron Hudson IIIs, all loaded with ten 100lb bombs began to take off at 2320hrs. Crewed entirely by Dutch personnel of the Royal Netherlands Naval Air Service, the squadron was both familiar with the Hudson and operating from its Norfolk base, which very often took them close or over their home country. All four Hudsons *en route* to the target experienced heavy flak from Terschelling onwards which was first landfall and nearly 150 miles from the target. The crew of V9058 'L' with D Schröder at the controls suffered a port engine failure but, after descending to 3,000ft, the unit fired up again by which time a decision had been made to bomb Wilhelmshaven instead. The crew of T9396 'P' also bombed Wilhelmshaven and the last hour and half of their sortie was flown on one engine all the way back to Bircham Newton. The remaining two managed to bomb Bremen but, like so many other crews, could not confirm where their bombs had fallen due to the weather conditions.

Just like all of the other aircrew taking part in *Millennium II*, those of 407 (Demon) Squadron were very keen to find out what the target was to be that night. Their commanding officer, Wg Cdr A C Brown DSO, DFC, divulged nothing, simply because he did not know either but when the 'Special Equipment' needed to attack shipping was removed from the squadron's Hudsons, they all knew that a bombing raid was in the offering and it was potentially a big one. There was much excitement in the air when eleven crews were selected for that night's operation which was revealed to them at the briefing by Bircham Newton's station commander who announced '…we are going to obliterate Bremen.' At 2320hrs, 407 Squadron was led away from Bircham Newton at 2320hrs by Wg Cdr Brown and crew on a route which was familiar to all until they headed inland from Terschelling which greeted them with a barrage of flak. Flying at 12,000ft, there was little to see below due to the cloud and it was only evident that Bremen was ahead because of a ring of exploding flak. Only six of the eleven crews claimed to have bombed Bremen. The odds of them actually hitting the assigned target of the Deschimag shipyard were slim, with the exception of one crew who descended to 7,000ft, found a break in the cloud and bombed the docks (there are many in Bremen) followed by explosions and fire. Wg Cdr Brown's crew ran short of fuel and were forced to turn back early 60 miles short of the target; as were Sqn Ldr W B Cooper's crew. 35 miles short of Bremen, Cooper decided to turn back as the target could not be located because of 10/10ths cloud. After steering north and jettisoning their bombs into the sea, the Hudson was attacked by what was thought to be a Bf 109. The fighter appeared to distract the crew by firing red flares and instantaneously a second enemy fighter attacked from below. The upper/rear gunner of the Hudson, Plt Off W H Brown, quickly responded by firing 150 rounds at the enemy aircraft before it rapidly disappeared. Brown was convinced that he had damaged the fighter and staked his claim after they had safely returned to Bircham Newton. Plt Off C H Bryan's aircraft was also attacked by an enemy machine using white tracer but no damage was caused and, all eleven of 407 Squadron's Hudsons made it back to their Norfolk home.

The main force strikes

Another future Pathfinder unit could do little about the conditions over Bremen and, of the 16 Stirlings detailed by 7 Squadron, at least five either failed to reach or to find the target. It was a slightly different picture for the 17 Halifaxes of 78 Squadron, the first of whom was over the target at 0123hrs and the last at 0206hrs. Of the 16 that got away from Middleton St George, 13 of them bombed but no results were observed by any crew. One crew, that of Fg Off J A Whittingham in Halifax II, W1067, was shot down by a night fighter of 2./NJG2 flown by Uffz Heinz Vinke and crashed at 0042hrs into the Ijsselmeer. Two of them, including Whittingham, were killed, while the remainder managed to bail out into captivity.

Having departed Balderton at 2255hrs, the first of 14 408 Squadron Hampdens reached Bremen at 0138hrs. However, by that time they were down to 13 as one aircraft was forced to return early with excessive vibration from the starboard engine. Two more were unable to establish a pin-point and turned back while the remaining eleven Hampdens dropped their bombs into the built-up area of the surrounding town of Bremen. It is also interesting to note that 408 Squadron recorded in their ORB that the attack on Bremen was made from the east on a heading of 295° rather than from the west which appears to be the route taken by the rest of the force. For example, the route flown by the Wellingtons of 103 Squadron out of Elsham Wolds was; 'Base, Mablethorpe – DR Position on Dutch Coast – Target – leaving target to Northerly DR position northwest of Borkum and then to Mablethorpe and Base'.

This was effectively a straightforward route direct to the target and once bombed, all aircraft would turn away to port and be over the sea again once clear of Frisian Islands. 103 Squadron reported heavy and light flak *en route* to the target while searchlight activity over Bremen was on a small scale. Of the 15 aircraft detailed, 13 of them bombed through solid cloud between 0139 and 0214hrs while two other crews bombed Vegesack and Cuxhaven.

Loaded with a pair of 500lb GP bombs and 360 x 4lb IBs apiece, the first of a dozen 420 Squadron Hampdens Is was led away from Waddington by its

commanding officer, Wg Cd D A R Bradshaw, in P1257 'C'. Over the target at the same time as 103 Squadron, all managed to bomb on ETA but, like those who had already attacked, were unable to confirm exactly where their bombs had fallen. Plt Off L S Anderson and crew in AE422 'J' summed up his sortie by stating, 'We were unable to get an accurate pinpoint, at any time during the trip due to 10/10ths cloud but bombed on ETA, nearby fires and S/Ls.' Flt Sgt S J Cybulski and crew in AT132 'U' had a brush with an unidentified enemy aircraft just as they entered the target area but luckily manage to evade it. WO E F Pinney, at the controls of AE378 'R', gave a detailed description of large fires burning in the town, while the target area was completely obscured by cloud. He spotted a pair of Bf 110s in the target area; one of them attempted to intercept his Hampden but quick evasive action prevented the night fighter firing.

Uffz Heinz Vinke of 2./NJG2 who claimed his third victory when he shot down Fg Off J A Whittingham's Halifax II over Holland en route to Bremen. Vinke went on to achieve 54 aerial victories, all at night, before he was killed in April 1944.

The first 17 Halifax IIs contributed by 405 Squadron were led away from Pocklington at 2304hrs by Sqn Ldr Thiele. This future Pathfinder unit flew its operation in two 'phases'; 'Phase 1'

The Thousand Bomber Raids

consisted of nine aircraft loaded with three 1,000lb time-delay bombs and nine SBCs filled with 90 x 4lb IBs, all carrying cameras. 'Phase 2', made up of the remaining six aircraft were loaded with three 1,000lb time-delay bombs, nine SBCs with 90 x 4lb IBs and a further eight 30lb IBs without cameras. The first of 405 Squadron's Halifaxes began bombing at 0126hrs and, by the time their part of the raid was over at 0235hrs, 13 aircraft had claimed to have bombed the primary despite the solid cloud conditions. Individual actions included Sqn Ldr Thiele and crew who bombed from 14,000ft at 0134hrs and were convinced that they had hit the dock area. A large fire was observed in that area and at 0138hrs, a searchlight was shot out by one of Thiele's gunners before he turned for home. Wg Cdr J E Fauquier DFC was the last to bomb at 0235hrs from 14,000ft, he then dived down over the city to as low as 100ft. The Halifax was quickly illuminated by a pair of searchlights and then engaged by a pair of light flak guns which were fired back at by the air gunners in the mid-upper and rear turrets resulting in one enemy gun falling silent and one searchlight being doused.

The Manchester's last show

Millennium II was destined to be the last operation that the much maligned Avro Manchester would take part in and it was a typically inauspicious start. 61 Squadron's Flt Sgt C P Shriner and crew in Manchester I, L7477 was the first aircraft away from Syerston at 2305hrs followed by one other Manchester and 13

Although Manchester I, L7277 was on the strength of 1654 CU at Wigsley at the time of Millennium II, *the aircraft was operated by Sgt D Gray and crew from 50 Squadron for the operation.*

405 Squadron, Handley Page Halifax II, W7710 'R' which took part in all three operations. For Cologne and Essen the bomber was flown by Plt Off Higginson and crew and for Bremen Sqn Ldr Thiele was the lead crew away from Pocklington. Via Tony Buttler

Lancasters. Shriner's sortie was destined to be short; intercom failure forced the bomber to turn back for home as they approached the Dutch coast. Flt Sgt F Hobson in the second Manchester, R5835, was also forced to turn back when oxygen equipment failed at 16,000ft; both aircraft were back on the ground at Syerston again at 0100 and 0125hrs respectively. For the Lancaster element, the raid continued with few incidents other than for Flt Sgt P W Gregory and crew in Lancaster I, R5869 who were struck by an incendiary whilst leaving the target at 14,000ft. The elevator was partially jammed as a result but, along with the remainder of the squadron, Gregory made it home safely.

The next Manchester-equipped unit to head for Bremen was 50 Squadron which was, by some margin, the largest operator of the twin-engine bomber and, for *Millennium II*, had detailed a dozen of them, plus a pair of Lancasters. Fg Off H W Southgate was the first to take-off from Skellingthorpe at 2307hrs in Manchester I, L7294. The usual round of failures occurred *en route* including Flt Sgt J F Taylor and crew in L7455 when their rear turret was found to be unserviceable forcing another early return. Another involved one of the two Lancasters flown by Flt Lt G A Wilkins when the starboard inner cut at 0001hrs while surprisingly, the remaining group of eleven Manchesters and one Lancaster continued to the target. However, another Manchester, R6769, flown by Plt Off H B Martin (later to become an Air Marshal and receive a knighthood), was also forced to turn back through rear turret failure but still took the opportunity to drop its incendiaries on Alkmaar airfield before heading home. Over the target, only one Manchester claimed to have identified the primary target while the remainder bombed through the cloud with the exception of Fg Off H W Southgate who dropped his bombs from just 2,500ft. Between them, the 50 Squadron aircraft are credited with dropping 556 x 30lb IB, 8,370 x 4lb IB and a single 4,000lb GP bomb the latter from the Lancaster of Fg Off N Goldsmith from 6,000ft. One aircraft had been lost; Manchester I, L7289 flown by Sgt J C Roy RNZAF and crew, which was hit by flak over Bremen, killing all seven crew. This was the last operational loss of an Avro Manchester in Bomber Command service.

49 Squadron were going through the transitional stages of re-equipping from the Manchester to the Lancaster and, as such, could only provide three of the former and one of the latter for *Millennium II* despite seven aircraft being detailed. Sgt J W Heard led the trio of Manchesters away from Scampton at 2322hrs in L7453 while the sole Lancaster, R5850, did not take off until 0002hrs. Ironically for this final Manchester operation, it was the Lancaster, flown by Commanding Officer, Wg Cdr L C Slee that suffered a hydraulics failure and, half an hour later, was back down on the ground. Of the Manchesters, all made it to Bremen and bombed the town rather than the cloud-covered primary and, more importantly, they all made it safely back to Scampton without a single unserviceability.

106 Squadron was in the same position as 49 Squadron regarding re-equipping but could muster 17 Lancasters and a pair of Manchesters. Because of their inferior performance the two Manchesters left Coningsby first at 2325 and 2330hrs respectively. 106 Squadron found the target to be no less clear than any other squadron but 18 of the 19 aircraft involved dropped their bombs in the target area, including the two Manchesters. Lancaster I, R5680, flown by Flt Lt J V Hopgood, also destined to take part in the dams raid with 617 Squadron, was forced to turn back early when both starboard engines cut as they crossed the Dutch coast. The bombs were jettisoned and with great skill, the bomber was brought home to Coningsby on the remaining two port engines. Taxying in at 0550hrs, Sgt S E J Jones and crew had carried out the final Manchester operation and, despite encountering a Ju 88 and a Bf 109 on their way home, had lived to tell the tale.

Night fighter harvest

The Pratt & Whitney Twin Wasp-powered Wellington IV was one of the better performing examples of the breed, certainly from a maximum speed point of view.

RAF Lindholme's 43-year old station commander, Gp Capt S J Skarzynski who was drowned after the 305 Squadron Wellington he was flying in ditched in the North Sea off Great Yarmouth.

460 Squadron mustered 20 of them for *Millennium II* and the first departed Breighton at 2305hrs in the hands of Wg Cdr A L G Hubbard DFC in Z1461 'D'. The majority of the 460 Squadron crews dropped their bombs through the cloud while others, including Sqn Ldr R B Osborne DFC, brought his bombs home later saying 'I did not consider it worthwhile to attack any defended area through 10/10 cloud.......'. Plt Off J Falkiner and crew in Wellington IV, Z1384 'F' were one of those crews who bombed at 0153hrs from 13,000ft. At 0230hrs, the crew were over Nordeney, on a heading of 311° and for some unknown reason at the low altitude of just 2,000ft. Suddenly, an aircraft was sighted approaching from the starboard quarter at a distance of 500 yards. Identified as an enemy machine the rear gunner, Sgt Witney DFC verified that it was a Ju 88 as tracer fire slipped above and below his turret. Closing to 200 yards, the Ju 88 manoeuvred into the starboard half-quarter of the Wellington and let rip with a long burst of fire. Falkiner flung the bomber into a steep dive to starboard forcing the Ju 88 to cross the tail of the Wellington which gave Witney the opportunity to fire a couple of bursts. Following the second burst of fire, flames were spotted coming from the starboard wing root of the Ju 88. Diving away, the Ju 88 was seen to slip through a gap in the clouds before crashing into the sea; Witney claimed it destroyed. It was not over yet for the Falkiner crew, whilst only 25 miles west of Nordeney at 0237hrs but at 6,500ft, a Bf 109 was spotted passing in front of the bomber on a southerly course. Once again, this appears to be a distraction technique as the Bf 109 was seen to have a white light in the middle of the nose and, moments after it passed, a second Bf 109 was spotted closing for an attack. As the Bf 109 approached to within 400 yards astern and approximately 600ft above, Witney opened fired again at 300 yards forcing the enemy fighter to break off and disappear into the clouds.

The Stirlings of 214 Squadron out of Stradishall had a mixed evening and, of the eleven taking part seven attacked the primary target, three returned early and another landed away. Bremen was attacked between 0126 and 0225hrs and

11,340 x 4lb IBs were dropped through 9/10ths and 10/10ths could. The Stirling of Plt Off Smith and crew, W7528 'T', was singled out by the night fighters beginning with a Bf 109 which the gunners managed to see off and possibly destroy moments before a second machine, a Bf 110, also attacked. The Bf 110's burst of fire was accurate and both the front gunner and flight engineer were wounded and the port outer engine was put out of action to such a degree that the entire propeller fell away. With injured crew on board, Smith opted for the nearest safe haven on return and landed at Coltishall.

Another squadron that would suffer at the hands of the night fighter was 218 Squadron who contributed 14 Stirlings, led away from Marham by Flt Sgt Boyd and crew in N3720 'B' at 2310hrs. *En route* to the target, Plt Off B F Ball and crew in W7503 'R' were attacked by Oblt Ludwig Becker of 6./NJG2. The bomber plunged into Wieringermeer Polder on the edge of the Ijsselmeer with the loss of all seven crew. Sgt R Waters and crew in Stirling I, DJ974 'T' had a hairy moment when their aircraft was hit by flak. Both starboard engines stopped running and the big bomber entered a spin from which Smith eventually recovered. The bombs were jettisoned into the sea and flak had also punctured a petrol tank which rapidly drained itself. Somehow, Smith managed to get his bomber back to Marham with no further drama but, sadly for him and his crew, tragedy was just round the corner. Two nights later, during a return raid to Bremen in the same aircraft, Waters and his crew were hit by flak again but this time there was no recovery and all seven crew were killed when the bomber crashed into the sea off Hohenstiefersiel.

149 Squadron's troubles began early at Lakenheath when Stirling I, R9330, one of ten detailed, with Flt Sgt Hockley at the controls, swung badly on take-off

Wg Cdr S M Krzyztyniak's 301 Squadron Wellington IV, Z1479 'A' in the mud off Dornumergrode on June 26, 1942.

following a failure of the starboard outer engine and crashed. Of the eight crew on board, all escaped injury bar one while the Stirling was written off following a fire. Of the remaining nine aircraft, seven managed to reach the target bombing on T.R. but failed to see the results of their efforts. *En route*, Plt Off C W Simmons in BF310 'H' had a brief brush with a Bf 110 and was forced to jettison 270 x 4lb IBs over the sea in order to regain stability and then proceeded to the target. Another aircraft, BF311 flown by WO F Ashbaugh, was forced to return early because of rear turret failure while Plt Off A Austin and crew in N6079 'F' also had a tussle with a Bf 110 west of Bremen. The Bf 110 attacked several times and at one point the rear gunner, Sgt J Barritt's machine guns jammed but, instead of panicking, displayed 'great coolness' during the whole engagement and the night fighter was forced to give up its quarry.

As with the two previous 'Thousand Plan' operations, the Polish crews of 305 (Wielkopolska) Squadron at Lindholme were very keen to strike again at the heart of Germany. The first of 15 crews took off at 2315hrs; the lead aircraft flown by Flt Lt E Rudowski in Wellington II, Z8528 which had amongst its crew members Lindholme's 43-year old station commander, Gp Capt S J Skarzynski. 14 of 305 Squadron's Wellingtons reached Bremen and bombed through dense cloud and all reported seeing a large number of fires across the target area. Only one aircraft was forced to turn back and that was Rodowski's Z8528 when the port Merlin engine stalled over the Dutch coast. The bombs were jettisoned and a course was set to base but, despite the Wellington II being more than capable of flying on one engine with a light load, could not maintain height. At approximately 0200hrs, the Wellington was ditched into a rough sea 14 miles off Great Yarmouth without injury to the five crew. The navigator successfully deployed the aircraft's dinghy but while the airmen were in the water a large wave struck the side of the aircraft which swept Gp Capt Skarzynski further out to sea. Despite their best efforts, the remaining four crew in the dinghy could not make head way towards their station commander and for 30 minutes they could hear his calls for help but could do little to him. The four men spent a further eight hours in the dinghy before they were rescued by a British warship. Sadly, Skarzynski's body was later washed up on the island of Terschelling where he is buried today.

Another Polish unit fired up for another crack at the enemy was 300 Squadron at Ingham which managed to prepare 13 Wellington IVs. With a footnote in the squadron ORB stating 'To cause maximum damage to the aiming point in Bremen Area' the raid turned out to be a disappointment for the Poles despite all 13 bombers reaching and attacking the target. The same frustration of being greeted by near solid cloud was experienced despite some aircrew observing many fires through small gaps in the cloud. It is also interesting to note that 305 Squadron was also approaching Bremen from an easterly direction. Plt Off S Machej and crew in Z1407 'Z' dropped on ETA from 17,000ft at 0205hrs on a heading of 270°. Unable to see the results of their bomb run, Machej descended to 3,000ft to take a closer look and was greeted with a number of extensive fires. All 13 crews made it safely home to Ingham but it was a close run thing for Plt Off H Kaluzny and crew in Z1415 'X'. Whilst flying over Dokkum at 12,000ft and with the North Sea clearly in sight a Bf 110 sneaked up on them and in a quick burst of accurate fire damaged the rear turret, the hydraulic system (which made the bomb bay doors open and stay open) and the port wing structure. Regardless, Kaluzny made his escape and landed back at Ingham without further trouble.

Fg Off P 'Peter' Tobolski, the observer from 301 Squadron, Wellington IV, Z1479, who along with his colleagues became a POW. Tobolski was one of the 76 who took part in the 'Great Escape' and one of 50 who were re-captured and shot.

Another Polish unit, 301 Squadron, operating out of Hemswell, despatched 14 Wellington IV, all of which managed to bomb the target area through the obligatory cloud. In such conditions, the odds of being hit by flak were reduced but this did not apply to the aircraft of the squadron's commanding officer, Wg Cdr S M Krzyztyniak and his crew, in Z1479 'A'. Whilst at 16,000ft over the target, the bomber was struck by flak, forcing the crew to take to their parachutes. It is possible that Krzyztyniak stayed (along with some, if not all of his crew) with his aircraft as photographic evidence shows Z1479 in one piece after crash landing off Dornumergrode, 65 miles northwest of Bremen. Regardless, all six were taken prisoner, including 38 year old observer, Fg Off P 'Peter' Tobolski, who was incarcerated in Stalag Luft 3. Tobolski was one of 76 men who managed to get out of the prison camp on March 25, 1944 during the famous 'Great Escape' only to become one of the 50, and one of six Poles, who were murdered by the Gestapo on April 2.

18 Wellington IIIs of 115 Squadron began leaving Marham at 2325hrs but only a dozen of them would locate the target due to a combination of T.R. and D.R. fixes and the tell-tale glow of fire beneath the 10/10ths cloud. Of the remainder, two aircraft brought their bomb loads home because the they could not find the target, a third partly jettisoned and brought back the remainder while Plt Off W L Croxton and crew in Wellington III, X3554 failed to return. The bomber was on the final leg when it crashed into the sea with the loss of all five crew and, as such, it can be presumed that they also managed to bomb the target. BJ589 'X', with Flt Lt T L

The final resting place of Sgt W A McCann RCAF of 115 Squadron in Marham Cemetery who succumbed to his injuries on June 28, 1942; the last RAF casualty of the 'Thousand Plan'. Author

Sandes at the controls, was attacked by an enemy aircraft over the target at 14,500ft but still manage to either drop or jettison its bomb load into the northern area of Bremen. The bomber was badly shot up and the rear gunner, Sgt W A McCann RCAF, was seriously wounded. The Wellington made it back to Marham but the 20 year old McCann succumbed to his injuries on June 28.

Now rid of its Manchesters, Waddington-based 44 Squadron was an all-Lancaster unit and would remain so until late 1945. Twelve Lancasters departed Waddington at 2329hrs, the first of them, R5631 'J', with Sqn Ldr D J Penham DSO, DFC in the captain's seat. Nine Lancasters managed to bomb Bremen, including Penham who delivered six 1,000lb GP bombs and 270 x 4lb IBs with the help of *GEE*. Of those that did not make it Bremen, Flt Lt Maudslay DFC and crew in R5862 'G' had by far the toughest trip. At 0131hrs at 16,000ft and approximately twelve miles southwest of Oldenburg, the bomber was hit by flak. Undeterred, Maudslay continued to the target but, on reaching it, the bomb doors failed to open and nothing would budge them. They were eventually manually pumped open by the crew but by this time they were off Borkum and the bombs were jettisoned safe into the sea. The earlier flak burst had caused more damage than had been realised mainly around the area of the port engines, including shattered hydraulic lines, failed temperature and pressure gauges not to mention a puncture of the central port fuel tank and an unserviceable rear turret. On top of that, the port inner began to vibrate forcing a shut down and a feathering of the propeller but Maudslay still got his crew and aircraft back home, although a precautionary landing was made at Cranwell rather than Waddington.

The Canadians of 419 (Moose) Squadron operating out of Mildenhall had already contributed to the previous raids to Cologne and Essen and, for Bremen, stumped up another 17 Wellingtons. Under the command of the popular Wg Cdr J 'Moose' Fulton, DSO, DFC, all but three managed to find and bomb Bremen. Sqn Ldr Wolfe and crew in Wellington III, X3360 dropped 810 x 4lb IBs on a T.R. fix and like saw many other crews saw a large red glow through the dense cloud and many good fires were burning. As the bomber settled in for the homeward trip, a night fighter was encountered at 0203hrs at 4,200ft, north of Borkum. It appears that the attacking Bf 110 stood little chance against the guns of rear gunner Sgt Morrison whose burst of fire struck the port engine of the night fighter which burst into flames. With the entire port wing ablaze, the Bf 110 plunged into the sea leaving only a ring of fire on the surface.

It had been a busy few weeks for 158 Squadron, having moved from Driffield to East Moor on June 6 and then converting from the Wellington II to the Halifax II. *Millennium II* would be the first operation with their new aircraft and 14 aircraft were detailed. It was an inauspicious start as three Halifaxes

The popular Wg Cdr J 'Moose' Fulton DSO, DFC, AFC, who was commanding officer of 419 (Moose) Squadron from December 21, 1941 until July 29, 1942.

failed to even start their engines because of a variety of technical issues. Led by their commanding officer, Wg Cdr P Stevens DFC and crew in Halifax II, W7745 'K' at 2336hrs, the target was reached at 0203hrs. Stevens, unbeknown to him at the time had his aircraft hit by flak on the run in, severing a small wire which caused an electrical failure and, as a result, the bomb load would not release. Unable to even jettison the load, a frustrated Stevens returned to East Moor with just a few holes as reward for a near six-hour sortie. Sgt White and crew in W1166 'L' were attacked by a night fighter *en route* and were forced to bomb what they thought to be Oldenburg instead. The enemy aircraft had caused a great deal of damage including a shredded hydraulic system, a shattered wireless set and even the dinghy had been blown out. Despite the delicate condition of his aircraft, White brought it home. 158 Squadron's first loss of a Halifax II came sooner than planned as Plt Off Bradbury in DG225 'N' ran short of fuel and was forced to ditch into the sea half a mile off Scarborough at 0530hrs. A common place for aircraft to ditch during the Second World War, all eight crew were rescued uninjured in a short period of time.

June 25, 1942 was an exciting day for 83 Squadron not only because they were about to learn that they would be taking part in another '...big do...' but also

83 Squadron aircrew being briefed on their route to Bremen at Scampton on June 25, 1942. RAF Scampton Heritage Centre

because the whole event was to be photographed from NFTs through to interrogation on June 26. One significant image that was taken during the briefing reveals the route that 83 Squadron was ordered to fly to the target. From a point south of Scampton, the 18 Lancasters detailed were to route out over Skegness and continue on the same course until the Dutch coast was crossed, north of Amsterdam (possibly Alkmaar region). It appears that then the bombers flew on a heading of 090° and then, after crossing the German border, steered approximately 075° direct to the target. Once bombed, the force was to turn due north for approximately ten miles and then turn to port, following a course which would take them back out over the sea in the region of Norden. This clarification of the route to the target may dispel some of the theories that the raid was directed from the east although that does not rule out the odd 'rogue' aircraft taking such a course, especially if their attack was being made at a much lower altitude than the main force. Of the 18 aircraft sent by 83 Squadron to Bremen at least 15 of them claimed

The Thousand Bomber Raids

One of many official press images of 83 Squadron preparing to depart for Bremen on the evening of June 25 at Scampton. The aircraft in the foreground is Lancaster I, R5620 'H' which was destined to be the only aircraft from 83 Squadron lost during the operation. RAF Scampton Heritage Centre

to have bombed the target while two others attacked Bremerhaven and Wilhelmshaven. A third aircraft, Lancaster I, R5620 flown by Plt Off J R Farrow RNZAF crashed at Winkelsett with loss of all eight crew.

The OTUs bear the brunt

For the hard-pressed OTUs, Bremen would be the final major operation that these vital training units would contribute to, although many other raids, certainly through to the end of 1942, had a number of OTU aircraft taking part. *Millennium II* would see the largest contribution yet seen from the OTUs and 16 of them would field at least 250 bombers for this last hurrah. This was all encouraging on paper for Harris who had already relied heavily on the both 91 and 92 (Training) Groups for the operations to Cologne and Essen and, on both occasions, the OTUs had performed well; in some cases, better than the squadron crews. Bremen would be a different kettle of fish for one significant reason; it was a lot further! For example, a round trip from Abingdon to Cologne was 760 miles (as the crow flies) while Bremen would be over 900 miles. This was not a massive difference but these were not state-of-the-art aircraft being flown by the OTUs, they were tired, battle-weary machines that did well to complete a navigation exercise let alone a long-distance raid with all the stresses and strains of carrying a full bomb load. With that in in mind, the OTUs would literally bear the brunt of the losses, thankfully for the final time.

Of the 50 Whitleys taking part in *Millennium II*, 48 of them were supplied by three OTUs; two of them, 10 and 19 OTU would operate from Abingdon. The latter had not taken part in a 'Thousand Plan' before and had made the long flight from its home base at Kinloss the previous day with twelve aircraft. 10 OTU, delivered yet again, this time fielding 20 Whitleys operated by a mixed bag of both green and seasoned crews while the 19 OTU machines were all flown by unit instructors with operational experience. For 10 OTU, 15 aircraft claimed to have successfully bombed Bremen while one crew was forced to turn back early following compass failure. Of the remaining four aircraft, there was no news and, back at Abingdon, the worst was feared. Sgt N M Oulster RCAF and crew in Whitley V, AD689, crashed near Lingen-Ems with the loss of all on board and none of the crew survived from Sgt E D Williams' RAAF crew in Whitley V, P4944 either; the latter coming down near Hamburg. BD201, with Sgt N R Parsons at the controls, was attacked by a night fighter of 2./NJG1 being flown by night fighter ace Hptmn Helmut Lent. The odds were clearly in the favour of the German pilot and the Whitley was brought down at 0300hrs near Wervershoof, only minutes away from reaching the North Sea and potential escape. On this occasion, four managed to bail out to become POWs while the bomb aimer, Sgt E George was possibly killed during Lent's attack. The fourth machine was luckier; Plt Off W W Colledge RCAF and crew in P5004 were forced to ditch in the North Sea and all five crew were rescued by an RAF High-Speed Launch. The Vancouver-born Colledge was awarded the DFC for his actions during this operation.

It is not known how 19 OTU fared over the target but one of their number did not return. Whitley V, Z6730, flown by Sgt J J Makarewicz and crew, were destined never to serve with an operational squadron; instead, the five-man crew spent the rest of the war in a POW camp.

A unit that contributed a number of Whitleys was another newcomer to the 'Thousand Plan'. 24 OTU at Honeybourne, east of Evesham, under the control of 7 Group, was still establishing itself during the Cologne and Essen operations but, by the time Bremen rolled around, unit strength was sufficient to detail 16 Whitley Vs for operations. Operating as 'B' and 'C' Flights, the former was to be led by Sqn Ldr L M Hodges and the latter by Sqn Ldr Wakefield. The raid itself appears to have gone well for 24 OTU and it is recorded that they dropped 50,494lb of 4lb IBs, 288 x 30lb IBs and 22 HE bombs on the target but as usual this result came at a price. One of the first units to take to the air for *Millennium II*, the first Whitley took off at

Whitley V, N1412 'O' of 19 OTU, one of a dozen contributed by the Kinloss and Forres-based training unit which for Millennium II, *operated from Abingdon.*

2215hrs and the last was away at 2306hrs, all with orders to land at Long Marston on their return which shortened their long journey by 50 miles for the return leg. Three Whitley's failed to return with the loss of all crews; these were Z9441 flown by Plt Off J A Preston RCAF and crew, BD266 flown by Sgt F M Cole RCAF (an all-pupil crew) which crashed off the Dutch coast and BD379 flown by Fg Off J B Monro RNZAF and crew which was last heard transmitting an SOS at 0411hrs. The signal was picked up by a direction station at Sealand over 400 miles away and the bomber was presumed to have crashed into the sea off the Frisian Islands. For those waiting at Long Marston for 24 OTU's return, the loss rate appeared initially to be much higher but there was some consolation when news came through that one aircraft had diverted to Coltishall and another to Aldermaston.

Both 11 and 12 OTUs, operating from Steeple Morden and Chipping Warden, contributed twelve and 20 Wellingtons respectively (although at least a dozen of the latter number may have operated from Snaith in company with 150 Squadron). Operating as 11 OTU 'Y' Sqn, three Wellington ICs failed to return including R1078 flown by Fg Off S G King RCAF which was loaded with a pair of 500lb GP bombs and three SBCs each loaded with 90 x 4lb IBs. The bomber was believed to have been brought down by a Bf 110 and crashed near Schale; King and his New Zealander rear gunner, WO W N Hollands were the only survivors. For 12 OTU's 20 Wellington ICs, it was another rough operation and it is not known how many came close to bombing Bremen. A number of skirmishes with night fighters were reported, including Plt Off Cowsill's DV952 which was attacked by a Ju 88 near Wilhelmshaven. Closing to 450 yards, the Wellington's rear gunner opened fire, resulting in the night fighter spinning away 'glowing red'; which was enough for a claim of 'probably destroyed.' The aircraft of Flt Lt Kerwan was also attacked by a Ju 88, approximately 45 miles northwest of Bremen but was successfully outmanoeuvred. Fg Off E J Cooper and crew in DV951 were not so lucky; they were shot down by a night fighter from 3./NJG1 at 0058hrs near Wietmarschen. It appears that all managed to bail out of the stricken bomber but one man, Sgt A P Read, succumbed to his injuries. Three other 12 OTU Wellingtons failed to return, two crashed into the sea with the loss of all on board while Sgt W J Bagley in Z8800 was forced to ditch 25 miles off Cromer from where they were picked up by a minesweeper. One of the lost Wellingtons was R1410 'M', flown by 18-year-old Sgt J T Shapcott; he was destined to be the youngest Bomber Command pilot to be killed in 1942.

14 OTU was another training unit which had consistently delivered in response to Harris' call and for *Millennium II* had detailed 24 Hampdens. On arrival, the crews found Bremen covered in solid cloud and almost impossible to identify. Despite this, 19 aircraft claimed to have bombed the city, with the remainder suffering various mechanical failings that caused at least one to dump its bomb load in the North Sea. One aircraft did not return, Hampden I, P5312 had already aborted the first two raids and fate struck the aircraft and its crew for a third time. The aircraft came down near Borkum, killing Flt Lt Count T E Salazar DFC and two of his crew instantly. Sgt H S Cusden, one of the air gunners, survived the crash only to die of his injuries in captivity a few days later. Salazar was a highly experienced instructor and was the son of the Count and Countess Demetria Salazar of Malvern in Worcestershire.

Of the remaining OTUs which took part, namely 15, 16, 18, 20, 21, 22, 23, 25 and 27 OTUs, all operating the Wellington with the exception of Finningley's 25 OTU, all lost aircraft. Whether it was a combination of the further distance involved and poor serviceability, the low loss 'enjoyed' by the OTUs during the Cologne and Essen operations was shattered over Bremen. A total of 30 OTU aircraft were lost, claiming the lives of 114 aircrew with a further 21 becoming POWs. 91 Group alone lost 23 bombers which equated to an alarming loss rate of 11.6%, over three times the acceptable figure. While the OTUs would continue to contribute to Bomber Command operations, they would never be called on for such a 'maximum effort' ever again, giving their trainee crews considerably more chance of actually surviving their operational training and allowing them to go on to serve on a squadron.

Damage on the ground

Despite the poor weather conditions which in part contributed to the damage caused to Bremen (thanks to an increasing wind which fanned the flames), the

The Thousand Bomber Raids

While Bremen escaped the same level of destruction caused to Cologne, by the end of the Second World War it looked no different as can be seen in this view taken in May 1945.

bombing caused a great deal of damage to the city and its infrastructure. The raid never stood any chance of equalling the devastation caused to Cologne but was considerably more effective than that caused to Essen. Many crews who could not identify the target bombed elsewhere including Borkum, Bremerhaven, Cuxhaven, Dorum, Emden, Hamburg, Lathan, Norden, Oldenburg, Vegesack and Wilhelmshaven. Other targets of opportunity included the airfields at Bergen/Alkmaar, Brussels, Groningen Elde, Leeuwarden and Liege.

With regard to the actual main objectives of *Millennium II*, 696 bombers claimed to have attacked but the Focke-Wulf Factory only suffered some serious damage to half a dozen buildings and not at the level that had been hoped for. One assembly shop was destroyed thanks to a single 4,000lb bomb delivered by a 5 Group Lancaster but this was not enough to disrupt production for too long. Neither the

A.G. Weser or Deschimag shipyards were damaged to any great degree but some industrial targets were hit. The damage caused can only be attributed to the use of *GEE* and the efforts of the first crews over the target with their flares. These included the Vulkan shipyard (U-boat production), Atlas Werke (producer of torpedoes, minesweepers and Enigma machines), Norddeutsche Hütte (steel production) and the Korff oil refinery.

It was the town of Bremen that suffered the most but not on a par with Cologne. 572 houses were flattened and 6,108 damaged, the majority of them in the eastern and southern areas of the town. 85 people were killed, almost 500 were injured and 2,378 were completely bombed out. Bremen had been incredibly lucky; the target had escaped due to unpredicted weather conditions but the RAF and eventually the 8th Air Force would continue to harass the area on 19 more major raids before the end of the war.

Harris would not find out exactly how his final 'Thousand Plan' operation had gone until the Mosquitoes of 105 Squadron set out again on a post-raid assessment operation. The AOC of Bomber Command would already have received a lot of feedback from his squadron commanders before their return, so the early news would not have been encouraging. The first two Mosquito IVs despatched at 0500 and 0527hrs from Horsham St Faith added to the frustration as both returned early with ASI and intercom failures respectively. Plt Off Down and Fg Off Skelton tried their hand at 1210hrs in Mosquito IV, W4069, returning at 1530hrs having photographed Hanover and a pair of airfields on their return journey. Full photographic evidence of the effect of the effects *Millennium II* was not achieved until Sgts Rowland and Carreck in DK292 left Horsham St Faith at 1424hrs, photographed Bremen from 24,000ft and were back on the ground at 1655hrs.

Bremen Losses

RAF Losses
1 (C)OTU** Hudson I, P5147; Crashed nr De Kooy – 4+
1 Sqn* Hurricane IIC, HL589; Lost on night intruder to Gilze-Rijen – 1+
7 Sqn Stirling I, N3754 'MG-O'; Shot down by night fighter, Lugthok – 4+ 3 POW
10 OTU Whitley V, P4944 'A'; FTR - 5+
Whitley V, P5004 'G'; Ditched in North Sea – All safe
Whitley V, AD689 'W'; Crashed Lingen-Ems – 5+
Whitley V, BD201 'L'; Shot down by night fighter, nr Wervershoof – 1+ 4 POW

11 OTU	Wellington IC, R1078 'TX-Q'; Shot down by Me110, nr Rheine – 3+ 2 POW
	Wellington IC, X3213 'KJ-L'; FTR – 5+
	Wellington IC, DV778 'KJ-A'; FTR – 5+
12 OTU	Wellington IC, R1349; Off Dutch coast – 5+
	Wellington IC, R1410 'KX-M'; Off Dutch coast – 5+
	Wellington IC, Z8800; Ditched off Cromer – All safe
	Wellington IC, DV951; Shot down by night fighter nr Bremen – 1+ 4 POW
13 Sqn	Blenheim IV, T2254 'A'; Shot down by night fighter, Aartselaar – 3+
	Blenheim IV, Z6084; Shot down by night fighter, Houwaart – 3+
14 OTU	Hampden I, P5312 'GL-J3'; Crashed Borkum – 3+ 1 inj
15 OTU	Wellington IC, DV737; FTR – 6+
	Wellington IC, DV935; Off Dutch coast – 6+
16 OTU	Wellington IC, X9982 'XG-A2'; FTR/LWT – 6+
18 OTU	Wellington IC, T2612 'H'; Attacked by night fighter, crashed nr Andijk – 5+
	Wellington IC, T2717 'C'; LWT – 5+
	Wellington IC, DV795 'N'; FTR – 5 POW
19 OTU	Whitley V, Z6730 'UO-Z'; FTR – 5 POW
20 OTU	Wellington IC, T2723; Hit by flak, crashed in sea – 3+ 2 POW
21 OTU	Wellington IC, X3179 'U'; LWT – 5+
22 OTU	Wellington IC, X9701 'D'; Ditched 50miles off Great Yarmouth – All safe
	Wellington IC, X9980 'K'; LWT – 5+
23 OTU	Wellington IC, X9875 'D3'; Lost off Dutch coast – 5+
	Wellington IC, DV475 'BY-G'; Shot down by night fighter, Azelo – 5+
24 OTU	Whitley V, Z9441; FTR – 5+
	Whitley V, BD266; Lost off Dutch coast – 5+
	Whitley V, BD379; FTR – 5+
26 OTU	Wellington IC, DV721 'N'; FTR – 5+
27 OTU	Wellington IC, R1162 'R'; LWT – 5+
35 Sqn	Halifax II, W1105 'TL-N'; Hit by flak, crashed nr Oldenburg – 5+ 2 POW
50 Sqn	Manchester I, L7289; Hit by flak, crashed Grembke – 7+
76 Sqn	Halifax II, W7747 'MP-G'; LWT – 7+
78 Sqn	Halifax II, W1067; Shot down by night fighter, Ijsselmeer – 2+ 4 POW
83 Sqn	Lancaster I, R5620 'OL-H'; Crashed at Winkelsett – 7+
102 CF	Halifax II, V9987 'DY-U'; FTR – 2+ 3 POW

102 Sqn	Halifax II, R9446 'DY-F'; Lost over sea – 6+
	Halifax II, W7654 'DY-Q'; Lost over sea – 6+
	Halifax II, W7759 'DY-L'; LWT – 6+
115 Sqn	Wellington III, X3554 'KO-Q'; Crashed into the sea – 5+
156 Sqn	Wellington III, BJ594; Crashed returning to Alconbury – 1 DOI
158 Sqn	Halifax II, DG225 'NP-H'; Ditched off Scarborough – All safe
206 Sqn**	Hudson, AM762 'S'; FTR – 5+
	Hudson, AM606 'M'; FTR – 3+ 2 POW
214 Sqn	Stirling I, W7538 'BU-T'; Crash-landed at Coltishall – 2 inj (by enemy action)
218 Sqn	Stirling I, W7503 'HA-R'; Shot down by night fighter, Wieringermeer – 7+
301 Sqn	Wellington IV, Z1479 'GR-A'; Hit by flak, crashed Bremen – 6 POW
304 Sqn**	Wellington IC, DV441; Shot down by night fighter in North Sea – 6+
305 Sqn**	Wellington II, Z8528 'SM-R'; Ditched 14 miles off Great Yarmouth – 1+
311 Sqn**	Wellington IC, Z1090 'Q'; Force landed at Brancaster Bay – All safe
1481 Flt	Wellington IC, X9812 'Z'; Lost off Dutch coast – 5+
1651 CU	Stirling I, W7442 'B'; Shot down by night fighter, Waddenzee – 7+
1652 CU	Halifax II, V9993 'GV-U'; Shot down by night fighter, Luttenberg – 2+ 5 POW
	Halifax II, R9372

*Fighter Command
**Coastal Command

Luftwaffe losses during the 'Thousand Plan'

Aircrafts losses and claims are a grey area with regard to the Luftwaffe, compared to the amount of reference material and detail available for RAF aircraft. Before we tackle the subject of air-to-air claims it must be remembered that a number of aircraft were destroyed or damaged on the ground during the intruder operations and a few more may have been added when bombers, who could not find their primary target, decided to drop their bombs on an enemy airfield instead. With regard to the intruder operations, despite obvious damage (and possibly destruction) being caused very few squadrons actually claimed any aircraft destroyed. It would be a conservative estimate that at least a dozen enemy aircraft were destroyed on the ground by the intruders alone, although more success could and should be gleaned by the disruption that these sorties caused.

In the air, three Ju 88s and one 'unknown' enemy night fighter were claimed during the Cologne operation; all of them to rear gunners. The Ju 88s were claimed by Halifaxes from 78 Squadron (destroyed) and 102 Squadrons, one destroyed and one probable respectively and another probable by a 23 OTU Wellington, while the 'unknown' was claimed destroyed, falling to the guns of Sgt H E De Mone RCAF in his 16 OTU Wellington.

During the Essen operation, six enemy aircraft were claimed, beginning with an 'unknown' probable by a 15 Squadron Stirling and another 'unknown' claimed destroyed by a 16 OTU Hampden. A 97 Squadron rear gunner, Sgt Ferguson was the only air gunner of the three operations to put in two claims when his 101 Squadron Wellington III, X3634, was attacked by enemy fighters. Rear gunner Ferguson shot a Bf 110 down and claimed to have damaged a Ju 88 as well. Another Ju 88 was claimed damaged by a 301 Squadron aircraft while the only other claim of the operation was Sgt Gawith of 1 Squadron who claimed a Ju 88 damaged. The latter claim turned out to be a destroyed.

During the Bremen operations, at least two Bf 110s and their crews were lost by the Luftwaffe that night while a Ju 88 was claimed destroyed by the rear gunner of a 12 OTU Wellington and a Bf 109 claimed damaged by the rear gunner of a 407 Squadron Hudson.

There is little doubt that the Luftwaffe suffered more damage in the air than the above 15 claims and in the heat of the moment, any damage caused during aggressive manoeuvring could be easily missed.

Reaping the whirlwind

For Arthur Harris, his goal had been achieved to put Bomber Command back squarely on the map after the success of the Operation *Millennium* to Cologne. There is no doubting that Bomber Command was in the doldrums with regard to being an effective cohesive force up to early 1942 and even prior to the trio of 'Thousand Plan' operations taking place during Harris's early tenure, advances had been made. Bomber Command would most likely have improved considerably thanks to new tactics and new equipment both from an aircraft and a navigation point of view but Harris needed to make a statement; firstly to his own Prime Minster and Chiefs of Staff and secondly to Hitler and thirdly, to the British people. The internal struggles of the senior staff of the Army, Navy and Air Force would continue until the end of the war but from June 1942 onwards Bomber Command would not be under the spotlight with regard to misdirected resources thrown at ineffective activities. With regard to Germany, whose Nazi leadership remained in complete denial as to the effectiveness of Bomber Command, the civilian population and an increasing number of the rank and file were beginning to realise that the war could be lost and their great nation was not as invincible as they had thought. While Bomber Command was an expensive force to field for the Allies, the cost of defending the Reich was something Hitler could have done without and the tens of thousands of personnel needed to defend Germany would ideally have served their Fuhrer more productively elsewhere.

The general feeling throughout Germany, certainly after Cologne, was if the RAF can cause this amount of devastation on their own, how could the country hold up when the Americans joined in. They would not have to wait long as the first official 8th Air Force operations began in August 1942 and with no let up until the end; the USAAF attacking during the day and the RAF, growing ever stronger, bombed at night.

A young force in its own right, Bomber Command was less than six years old when the 'Thousand Plan' was unleashed and during that time it had come a considerably long way from those peaceful pre-war biplanes. Harris's arrival and the fresh ideas he brought to Bomber Command was the equivalent of turning a wild horse into a thoroughbred. Behind the scenes, aircraft production was on the increase, training, thanks to the OTU system, was much improved, turning crews out an ever higher rate and the number of operational squadrons was also increasing and would continue to do so until the early days of 1945. The resources were there, backed up by manufacturing efficiency, all of which provided Harris and his group commanders with the tools they needed. Improved tactics such as the bomber stream resulted in much more concentrated, better organised operations which kept the loss rate to the absolute minimum. This new nocturnal formation flying would also be backed up by improved information at the initial crew briefing with individual aircraft allocated a specific time when they should be over the target and a route to follow which was only deviated from in an emergency. Operations would be further enhanced when the 'Master' bomber system was introduced which continued to control the entire raid as it evolved. The introduction of *GEE* as a navigation aid was another game changer, resulting in more accurate raids regardless of the weather. The use of a 'Shaker Force' or 'Marker Force' proved to be another way forward for more accurate raids and this specialist role at the head of an operation, would create a new group of its own operating as the 'Pathfinders'.

The aircraft that would see Bomber Command through to the end of war during the European war were present for the 'Thousand Plan', as were those that had been serving since the beginning. Of the aircraft taking part, the Blenheim, Hampden, Manchester, Stirling, Wellington and Whitley would all be withdrawn from Bomber Command's operational squadrons in the European Theatre long before the war's end while the Halifax, Lancaster and the Mosquito would provide the new backbone for the force until May 1945. Cologne would be the first time that the

Mosquito had been flown operationally over Germany and this highly versatile aircraft would go on to serve Bomber Command in ever increasing numbers proving to be ideal in the Pathfinder role.

In a feeble attempt to maintain civilian morale, the German propaganda machine tried to dismiss the idea that anywhere near 1,000 bombers were actually used during the three raids and with regards to Bremen for example, it was claimed that only 80 aircraft were involved and 52 of them had been shot down; the latter figure was only four over the actual amount while the former was nearly 900 under! The British, although to a slightly lesser degree, would also feed off the propaganda these huge raids created and the press had a field day just as Harris had hoped for, playing heavily on the number 1,000 and the devastation caused. The man in the street had always taken some solace in the fact that even at the beginning of the war Bomber Command had, at least, given the impression that Britain was striking back at Germany because of the RAF's physical presence, unlike the Royal Navy and Army who were fighting in distant seas or in foreign lands. The sight of Fighter Command during the day and the sound of Bomber Command at night went someway towards maintaining morale but when news of the damage caused in Cologne, its success and the only slightly less subdued news of the follow up raids, civilian morale began to rise in 1942 and never looked back until victory three years later. That year also saw victory in North Africa at El Alamein followed by the Germans' eviction from North Africa followed by equally encouraging news that the Soviets, albeit at great cost, had won the Battle of Stalingrad, both by early 1943. This was the real beginning of the end for Nazi Germany.

7

The Aircraft Involved in All Three Raids

Royal Air Force

Armstrong Whitworth Whitley V

One of the mainstays of Bomber Command during the early stages of the Second World War, the Whitley first entered RAF service in 1937 with 10 Squadron at Dishforth. The Whitley V flew its last bombing operation with 58 Squadron in late April 1942 but went on to serve with OTUs until the end of the war.

28 Whitley's were operated with 1481, 1483, 1484 and 1502 Flights during the Cologne operation; 29 operated with 10 OTU, 1481, 1484 and Flights for Essen and 50 were despatched by 10, 19 and 24 OTUs and possibly 1481 Flight for Bremen.

Crew: 5
Engines: Two 1,145hp Rolls-Royce Merlin X
Span: 84ft
Length: 70ft 6in
Weight (Max): 33,500lb
Weight (Empty): 19,330lb
Service Ceiling (At max weight): 17,600ft
Speed (Max): 222mph at 17,000ft
Speed (Cruise): 165mph at 15,000ft
Range (Max bomb load): 630 miles with 8,000lb bomb load or 1,930 miles and a 3,500lb bomb load with auxiliary fuel tanks
Armament: One .303in in front turret and four .303in in rear turret

The Thousand Bomber Raids

An Armstrong Whitworth Whitley V powers up one of its 1,145hp Rolls-Royce Merlin X engines. Over a hundred Whitley's took part in the 'Thousand Plan', all contributed by OTUs and various Flights. Via Tony Buttler

Avro Lancaster I

The most successful RAF bomber of the Second World War, the Lancaster first entered service with 44 Squadron in late 1941. It was not a prominent player in the 'Thousand Plan', although a number of Avro Manchester squadrons which were re-equipping with the type fielded both for the raids.

The Lancaster was operated by 44, 49, 50, 61, 83, 97, 106 and 207 Squadrons for all three operations, although only 97 and 207 Squadrons were fully equipped with the bomber for all three. 73 Lancasters were despatched for Cologne, 74 for Essen and 96 for Bremen.

Crew: 7
Engines: Four 1,280hp Rolls-Royce Merlin XX
Span: 102ft
Length: 69ft 6in

An icon of the Second World War, the Avro Lancaster was still finding its feet at the time of the 'Thousand Plan'. Via Tony Buttler

Weight (Max): 72,000lb
Weight (Empty): 36,900lb
Service Ceiling (At max weight): 20,000ft
Speed (Max): 287mph at 11,500ft
Speed (Cruise): 216mph at 20,000ft
Range: 1,660 miles with 14,000lb bomb load or 2,250 miles with a 10,000lb load
Armament: Two .303in in front turret; two .303in in mid-upper turret and four .303in in rear turret

Avro Manchester I

The story of the Manchester was all about the engines as the entire aircraft was designed around a pair of under-developed Vultures instead of the planned Merlins,

The Thousand Bomber Raids

The 'Thousand Plan' and in particular Millennium II *marked the end of the operational career of the Avro Manchester; very few tears were shed!*

which were all being diverted to fighters at the time; namely the Hurricane and Spitfire. The aircraft obviously had great potential and it first entered service with 207 Squadron in late 1940. With the engines behaving themselves the Manchester was capable enough, but was thankfully developed into the Lancaster and the rest is history.

The Manchester served in all three operations, but as they progressed, the bomber was detailed in ever decreasing numbers as it approached its withdrawal from service. For Cologne, 46 Manchesters operated with 44CF, 49 Squadron and CF, 50, 61, 83 and 106 Squadrons, 106CF and 408CF. For Essen the 33 Manchesters operated with 44CF, 44, 49, 50, 106 Squadron and CF and 408 Squadrons and finally Bremen which saw 20 of the type despatched by 49, 50, 61 and 106 Squadrons.

Crew: 7
Engines: Two 1,760hp Rolls-Royce Vulture
Span: 90ft
Length: 68ft 10in
Weight (Max): 50,000lb
Weight (Empty): 29,432lb
Service Ceiling (At max weight): 19,200ft

Speed (Max): 273mph at 17,000ft
Speed (Cruise): 185mph at 15,000ft
Range: 1,200 miles with 10,350lb bomb load or 1,630 miles with an 8,100lb load
Armament: Two .303in in front turret; two .303in in mid-upper turret and four .303in in rear turret

Bristol Beaufighter IC

Operated by Coastal Command as an anti-shipping strike fighter, the Beaufighter was a highly capable aircraft which served in ever progressing marks through the entire war. Tasked with carrying out night intruder patrols as part of Coastal Command's contribution to *Millennium II*, their numbers were limited. A total of ten Beaufighter ICs were contributed by 235 and 236 Squadrons.

Crew: 2
Engines: Two 1,400hp Bristol Hercules
Span: 57ft 10in
Length: 41ft 4in
Weight (Max): 21,000lb
Weight (Empty): 13,800lb
Service Ceiling: 29,000ft
Speed (Max): 330mph
Range: 1,500 miles
Armament: Four 20mm cannon in nose; six .303in in the wings and two 250lb bombs

Bristol Blenheim IV

One of the fastest light bombers in the world before the outbreak of the Second World War, the Blenheim bore the brunt of Bomber Command's daylight operations up to late 1941 and suffered high losses as a result. By 1942 the type was being replaced by the Boston, but continued to serve Bomber Command until August 1942. Well suited to the night intruder role, the Blenheims employed for the 'Thousand Plan' all served in this capacity.

Four Blenheim units, 13, 18, 114 and 614 (County of Glamorgan) Squadrons contributed aircraft to all three operations.

Crew: 3
Engines: Two 920hp Bristol Mercury XV
Span: 56ft 4in
Length: 42ft 7in

The Thousand Bomber Raids

The Bristol Blenheim played its part as an intruder in all three operations and for Millennium II, 20 of them were allocated the A.G. Weser shipyard as a target.

Weight (Max): 15,800lb
Weight (Empty): 9,790lb
Service Ceiling (At max weight): 22,000ft
Speed (Max): 266mph at 11,800ft
Speed (Cruise): 180mph at 15,000ft
Range: 1,460 miles with a max bomb load of 1,000lb
Armament: Two .303in in front; one .303in fixed under nose and two .303in in mid-upper turret

De Havilland Mosquito IV
One of the greatest combat aircraft of the Second World War, the high-performance Mosquito enhanced Bomber Command's capability by some margin. The Mosquito would remain the fastest aircraft in the Bomber Command inventory until the arrival of the jet-powered English Electric Canberra.

The Mosquito carried out its first Bomber Command operation over Germany when the first of four were despatched for post-raid assessment sorties to Cologne by 105 Squadron and a further three supported in an ASR capacity.

105 Squadron contributed three more aircraft for post-raid sorties to Essen. For Bremen, 105 Squadron were joined by 139 Squadron, both contributing a pair aircraft in an intruder role while the former despatched four aircraft for post-raid sorties.

Crew: 2
Engines: Two 1,250hp Rolls-Royce Merlin 21
Span: 54ft 2in
Length: 40ft 9½in
Weight (Empty): 14,600lb
Weight (Loaded): 20,870lb
Service Ceiling: 28,800ft
Speed (Max): 340mph at 22,000ft
Speed (Cruise): 300mph at 22,000ft
Range: 2,040 miles
Armament: 2,000lb bomb load

Douglas Boston III

The American-built Boston III was introduced into RAF service to replace the Blenheim in anti-shipping and daylight bombing role, mainly with 2 Group, although 11 Group also operated the type in the intruder role. The type entered service with 88 Squadron in February 1942 and remained in service until the end of the war.

It was in the intruder role that the type served in all three operations, 11 Group's 23 and 418 (City of Edmonton) Squadrons in all three and 2 Group's 88, 107 and 226 Squadrons bolstering the numbers for Bremen.

Crew: 3
Engines: Two 1,600hp Wright Cyclone GR-2600-A5B
Span: 61ft 4in
Length: 47ft
Weight (Max): 25,000lb
Weight (Empty): 15,650lb
Service Ceiling (At max weight): 24,250ft
Speed (Max): 304mph at 13,800ft
Speed (Cruise): 200mph at 15,000ft
Range: 1,240 miles with a max bomb load of 2,000lb
Armament: Four .303in in front; two .303in in mid-upper turret and four 20mm in a ventral position

The Thousand Bomber Raids

Douglas Havoc I
The Havoc was a name applied to the night fighter and intruder version of the Boston, which first entered service with 85 Squadron in April 1941. Only 40 Havocs ever served in the RAF making this a rare beast and for all three operations, the type only served with 23 Squadron in the intruder role.

Crew: 3
Engines: Two 1,200hp Pratt & Whitney Wasp S3C4-G
Span: 61ft 4in
Length: 47ft
Weight (Max): 19,040lb
Weight (Empty): 11,400lb
Service Ceiling (At max weight): 26,000ft
Speed (Max): 295mph at 13,000ft
Speed (Cruise): 210mph at 15,000ft
Range: 1,000 miles with a max bomb load of 3,000lb
Armament: Four .303in in front and one .303in Vickers 'K' in mid-upper turret

Handley Page Halifax II
The Halifax may have been the second four-engined 'heavy' to enter RAF service but it proved to be the first to drop bombs on Germany in March 1941. Production and entry into service was swift and by the time of the 'Thousand Plan' the Halifax was only second to the Wellington in numbers. Operating alongside the Lancaster, the Halifax would carry through Bomber Command's offensive against Germany to the end of the war by which time the type had flown 82,773 operational sorties. Without exception, all Halifaxes contributed to the 'Thousand Plan' were the Merlin-powered Mk II. For all three raids, aircraft were contributed by 10, 35, 76, 78, 102 and 405 Squadrons and 1652 CU while 158 Squadron, which converted from the Wellington, in time to operate the Halifax to Bremen.

Crew: 7
Engines: Four 1,280hp Rolls-Royce Merlin X
Span: 98ft 10in
Length: 70ft 1in
Weight (Max): 59,000lb
Weight (Empty): 34,500lb
Service Ceiling (At max weight): 18,000ft
Speed (Max): 262mph at 18,000ft
Speed (Cruise): 195mph at 15,000ft

78 Squadron Handley Page Halifax II, L9601 which took part in Operation Millennium *in the hands of Sgt Wilson and crew and* Millennium II *with commanding officer Wg Cdr Lucas at the controls.* Via Tony Buttler

Range: 1,000 miles with a max bomb load of 13,000lb or 2,720 miles with a 1,500lb bomb load

Armament: Four .303in in front turret; two .303in in mid-upper turret; four .303in in rear turret and four .303in in a ventral position

Handley Page Hampden I

Another aircraft that bore the brunt during the early stages of the war alongside the Wellington was the Hampden. It was described by its pilots as a bomber that flew like a fighter which was quite impressive considering it could deliver a 4,000lb bomb load. The Hampden continued to serve Bomber Command until September 1942 when 408 Squadron attacked Wilhelmshaven.

For the 'Thousand Plan' the Hampden was operated by 408 and 420 Squadrons and 14 and 16 OTUs although the latter was an all-Wellington operation for Bremen. 79 were despatched for Cologne, 71 for Essen and 50 for Bremen.

Crew: 4
Engines: Two 1,000hp Bristol Pegasus

The Thousand Bomber Raids

The Handley Page Hampden was officially classified as a medium bomber but its agility meant it performed more like a fighter. As a fighting machine, the Hampden was poor from a crew communication and co-operation point of view. Flight via Tony Buttler

Span: 69ft 2in
Length: 53ft 7in
Weight (Max): 22,500lb
Weight (Empty): 11,780lb
Service Ceiling (At max weight): 20,000ft
Speed (Max): 254mph at 13,800ft
Speed (Cruise): 155mph at 15,000ft
Range: 1,200 miles with a max bomb load of 4,000lb or 1,885 miles with a 2,000lb bomb load
Armament: Four .303in in front; one .303in in mid-upper position and one .303in in a ventral position

Hawker Hurricane IIC
One the best and most-underrated night intruder aircraft of the mid-war period was the cannon-armed Hurricane IIC. Its long range made it ideal for harassing targets

of opportunity deep into enemy territory and during the *Millennium II* one 1 Squadron plane flew as far west as Dusseldorf. As part of 11 Group's contribution to night intruder operations, Hurricanes of 1 and 3 Squadrons took part in all three 'Thousand Plan' operations.

Crew: 1
Engines: One 1,280hp Rolls-Royce Merlin XX
Span: 40ft
Length: 32ft
Weight (Max): 7,800lb
Weight (Empty): 5,800lb
Service Ceiling (At max weight): 35,600ft
Speed (Max): 339mph at 22,000ft
Range: 970 miles
Armament: Four 20mm Hispano cannon

Lockheed Hudson I, III*& V

The very first American-built aircraft to enter RAF service, the Hudson joined 224 Squadron at Leuchars in May 1939. Ideally suited to anti-submarine and general reconnaissance duties, the Hudson was a natural for service with Coastal Command. It was a Hudson that took the prize of being the first RAF aircraft to shoot down an enemy machine on October 8, 1939.

All 82 of the Hudsons that took part in *Millennium II* were from the following Coastal Command units; 1 (C)OTU, 59, 206, 224, 320 and 407 Squadrons.

Crew: 5
Engines: Two 1,200hp Wright Cyclone GR-1820-G205A (III)
Span: 65ft 6in
Length: 44ft 4in
Weight (Max):
Weight (Empty):
Service Ceiling: 24,500ft
Speed (Max): 255mph
Speed (Cruise): 223mph
Range (Max): 2,160 miles
Armament: Two fixed .303in in nose; two .303in in dorsal turret; one .303in in ventral position and provision for two .303in in beam position; max bomb load, 1,600lb

*Stats are for Mk.III

The Thousand Bomber Raids

With the capability of carrying up to a 1,600lb bomb load, the Lockheed Hudson's contribution from Coastal Command for Millennium II *could have made all the difference if the conditions had been better.*

Short Stirling I

The Stirling was the first four-engined monoplane aircraft to enter RAF service in August 1940 with 7 Squadron, then based at Leeming. The limitations of the Stirling are well documented thanks to a restrictive design criteria, but regardless of this, the aircraft was very popular with its crews. Considering its failures, which included a poor service ceiling, the Stirling did well to remain in Bomber Command service until September 1944.

The Stirling took part in all three operations with 7, 15, 149, 214 and 218 Squadrons and 1651 CU. 88 were contributed to *Millennium*, 77 to Essen and 69 to *Millennium II*.

Crew: 7
Engines: Four 1,425hp Bristol Hercules XI
Span: 99ft 1in
Length: 87ft 3in

A 149 Squadron Short Stirling I is manhandled by groundcrew at Lakenheath in 1942. The unit's aircraft contributed to all three operations.

Weight (Max): 70,000lb
Weight (Empty): 44,500lb
Service Ceiling (At max weight): 16,500ft
Speed (Max): 245mph at sea level
Speed (Cruise): 200mph at 15,000ft
Range: 740 miles with a max bomb load of 14,000lb or 2,330 miles with a 1,500lb bomb load
Armament: Two .303in in front turret; two .303in in mid-upper turret; four .303in in rear turret and four .303in in a ventral position

Vickers Wellington IA, IC, II, III & IV

More affectionately known as the 'Wimpey', the Barnes Wallis-designed geodetic Wellington was a huge success and without it at the beginning of the war, Harris's fear that Bomber Command could be dissolved would undoubtedly have already come to fruition by 1942. The Wellington was the only 'heavy', long-range bomber capable of delivering a sizeable bomb load until eventually superseded by the larger four-engined machines. The Wellington, which entered service in 1938, was not

The backbone of RAF Bomber Command and the backbone of all three 'Thousand Plan' operations. Without the Vickers Wellington, Bomber Command, as an independent force, would have possibly never existed during the Second World War.

withdrawn from Bomber Command operations until October 1943 by which time it had flown 47,409 sorties.

The Wellington's contribution to the 'Thousand Plan' was crucial and colossal; 602 were detailed for Cologne, 545 for Essen and 472 for Bremen serving with 9, 12, 57, 75, 101, 103, 109, 115, 142, 150, 156, 158, 300, 301, 305, 419 and 460 Squadrons, 1429 and 1483 Flights, 15 Squadron BATF, 11, 12, 15, 16, 18, 20, 21, 22, 23, 25, 26 and 27 OTUs and 1 AAS and the CGS.

Crew: 6
Engines: Two 1,000hp Bristol Pegasus XVIII (I); two 1,145hp Rolls-Royce Merlin X (Mk.II); two 1,500hp Bristol Pegasus; two 1,050hp Pratt & Whitney Twin Wasp R-183S3C4-C (Mk.IV)
Span: 86ft 2in
Length: 64ft 7in
Weight (Max): 28,500lb (IC)
Weight (Empty): 18,556lb (IC)
Service Ceiling (At max weight): 18,000ft (IC)
Speed (Max): 235mph at 15,500ft (IC); 299mph (Mk.IV)
Range: 1,540 miles with a 4,500lb bomb load or 2,200 miles with a 1,500lb bomb load (Mk.III)
Armament: Two .303in in front turret; two .303in in rear turret and two .303in in beam positions

Luftwaffe

Messerschmitt Bf 109E

A number of 'single-seat' fighters were reported by bomber crews during the three operations and these were most likely variants of the Messerschmitt Bf 109. As discussed at the beginning of this book, the Bf 109D was introduced to the night fighter role during the early stages of the war but would have been long removed from service by May 1942. With that in mind, it was most likely the Bf 109E which were spotted by the crews as the later 'F' was more common on the Eastern Front at the time.

Crew: 1
Engines: Daimler-Benz 601
Span: 32ft 4½in (E)
Length: 28ft 4½in (E)

Service Ceiling: 34,450ft (E)
Speed (Max): 354mph at 12,000ft (E)
Speed (Cruise): 300mph at 13,120ft (E)
Range: 410 miles (E)
Armament: One MG FF/M cannon firing through hub and 20mm MG FF cannons in wings (E)

Messerschmitt Bf 110D-3, E-1, E-2 & F-4a

By far the most common night fighter in service during May and June 1942 would have been the night fighter variants of the Messerschmitt Bf 110. The D-3 was a longer range version of the C model and remained in service until late 1943. Thanks to extra fuel tanks the D-3 could remain aloft for three hours. The E model entered service with several night fighter units from April 1941 and also remained until late 1943. Thanks to more powerful engines, the E model was the fastest of the breed even with the addition of a third crew member. The Bf 110E/U-1 was a modified night fighter which was equipped with the FuG 202 *Lichtenstein* B/C radar which was introduced in March 1942. The F model was a dedicated night fighter from the start unlike the D and E models. Faster, a greater range and potential to mount a

A Messerschmitt Bf 110F of 7./NJG 4 airborne near Juvincourt airfield in June 1942. Bundesarchiv

pair of 20mm MG FF upward-firing cannon (*Schräge Musik*) made this machine one of the best of the breed.

Crew: 2-3 (D & E); 3 (F)
Engines: Two Daimler-Benz DB 601A (D); two 1,250hp DB 601N (E); two 1,350hp Daimler-Benz DB 601F (F)
Span: 53ft 5in (F)
Length: 39ft 9in (F)
Weight (Max): 14,884lb (F)
Weight (Empty): 11,466lb (F)
Service Ceiling (At max weight): 35,760ft (F)
Speed (Max): 311mph at 14,760ft (F)
Speed (Cruise): 278mph at sea level (F)
Range: 744 miles (F)
Armament: Two 20mm, four 7.9mm (all forward-firing) and a single 7.9mm (rear cockpit) (F)

Junkers Ju 88C

The most significant night fighter unit which was equipped with the Junkers Ju 88 during the early stages of the was 2./NJG2, which was transferred to the Mediterranean in October 1941. Production of the Ju 88C continued through to

By far the most versatile aircraft in the Luftwaffe inventory, the Junkers Ju 88 served in all theatres throughout the entire war.

1942 and by the time of the 'Thousand Plan' at least 200 were in service. British intelligence at the time barely mentions the type, but as you will have read, the Ju 88 is constantly referred to in this book during many of the night fighter attacks. Some may have been misidentified but to report them so many times by so many crews must have put the type in service with a number of night fighter units in mid-1942 and C-2, C-4 or C-6 models (Data for C-6) are the most likely candidates.

Crew: 4
Engine: Two 1,159hp Daimler-Benz DB 601
Span: 59ft 0⅔in
Length: 51ft 9⅔in
Weight (Loaded): approx 12,000lb
Weight (Empty): approx 20,000lb
Service Ceiling: 32,472ft
Speed (Max): approx 314 mph at 14,764ft
Range (Max): approx 1,500 miles
Armament: Four 7.92mm MG 17 machine guns grouped in the upper nose and two 20mm FF cannon in the lower nose

Dornier Do 215B-5
Known as the 'Kauz III', a small number of Dornier Do 215B-1s and B-4s were converted with an IR searchlight in the nose and later the FuG 202 radar. At the time of the 'Thousand Plan' only a small number were in service, making this the rarest of all the night fighters at the time.

Crew: 4
Engine: Two 1,400hp Junkers Jumo 211J
Span: 65ft 10½in
Length: 46ft 10½in
Weight (Loaded): 27,232lb
Weight (Empty): 19,977lb
Service Ceiling: 32,472ft
Speed (Max): 307 mph at 17,384ft
Range (Max): 1,230 miles
Armament: Three 7.9mm MG 17 machine guns and one MG FF/M cannon grouped in the nose and a pair of forward firing cannon in a ventral gondola; 'Schräge Musik' comprising a pair of MG FF or MG 151 cannon

Bibliography

Action Stations Revisited No.1 by M J F Bowyer
Action Stations Volume 6 by M J F Bowyer
Aircraft of the RAF since 1914 by O Thetford
Avro Manchester by R Kirby
Cologne, The First 1,000-Bomber Raid by C Messenger
Combat Ready by A Goodrum
Fighter Command Losses – 1942 by N Franks
Luftwaffe Night Fighter Combat Claims 1939-45 by J Foreman, J Matthews and S Parry
Nachtjagd by T Boiten
RAF Bomber Command Losses – 1942 by W R Chorley
RAF Bomber Command Losses – HCUs & Miscellaneous Units by W R Chorley
RAF Bomber Command Losses OTUs – 1940-47 by W R Chorley
RAF Flying Training & Support Units by R Sturtivant
The Bomber Command War Diaries – An Operational Reference Book by M Middlebrook & C Everitt
The Cinderella Service by A Hendrie
The Thousand Plan by R Barker

National Archives

AIR 14/3507 (Harris correspondence with PM) - National Archives
AIR 27/3 (1 Sqn), 27/33 (3 Sqn), 27/99 (7 Sqn), 27/126 (9 Sqn), 27/143 (10 Sqn), 27/166 (12 Sqn), 27/181 (13 Sqn), 27/203 (15 Sqn), 27/244 (18 Sqn), 27/287 (23 Sqn), 27/379 (35 Sqn), 27/449 (44 Sqn), 27/481 (49 Sqn), 27/487 (50 Sqn), 27/538 (57 Sqn), 27/555 (59 Sqn), 27/577 (61 Sqn), 27/646 (75 Sqn), 27/650 (76 Sqn), 27/660 (78 Sqn), 27/686 (83 Sqn), 27/716 (88 Sqn), 27/766 (97 Sqn), 27/802 (101 Sqn), 27/808 (102 Sqn), 27/814 (103 Sqn), 27/826 (105 Sqn), 27/832 (106 Sqn), 27/843 (107 Sqn), 27/853 (109 Sqn), 27/882 (114 Sqn), 27/889 (115 Sqn), 27/960 (139 Sqn), 27/973 (142 Sqn), 27/1002 (149 Sqn), 27/1010 (150 Sqn), 27/1041 (156 Sqn), 27/1048 (158 Sqn), 27/1223 (206 Sqn), 27/1233 (207 Sqn), 27/1321 (214 Sqn), 27/1350 (218 Sqn), 27/1387 (224 Sqn), 27/1406 (226 Sqn), 27/1443 (235 Sqn), 27/1447 (236 Sqn), 27/ 1656 (300 Sqn), 27/1660 (301 Sqn), 27/1668 (304 Sqn), 27/1672 (305 Sqn), 27/1687 (311 Sqn), 27/1713 (320 Sqn), 27/1787 (405 Sqn), 27/1794 (407 Sqn), 27/1796 (408 Sqn), 27/1820 (418 Sqn), 27/1822 (419 Sqn), 27/1825 (420 Sqn), 27/1907 (460 Sqn), 27/2120 (614 Sqn)
AIR 28/670 & 671 (27 OTU)
AIR 50/483 (23 OTU combat claim)

Abbreviations & Glossary

AACU	Anti-Aircraft Co-operation Unit
AAS	Air Armament School
AMES	Air Ministry Experimental Station
AOC	Air Officer Commanding
ARP	Air Raid Precautions
ASI	Air Speed Indicator
BATF	Blind Approach Training Flight
BDU	Bombing Development Unit
CF	Conversion Flight
CGS	Central Gunnery School
CO	Commanding Officer
(C)OTU	(Coastal) Operational Training Unit
CU	Conversion Unit
DOI	Died of Injuries
E/A	Enemy Aircraft
ETA	Estimated Time of Arrival
EVD	Evaded
Fg Off	Flying Officer
Flt	Flight
Flt Lt	Flight Lieutenant
Flt Sgt	Flight Sergeant
FTR	Failed to Return
GP	General Purpose
Gp Capt	Group Captain
HC	High Capacity
HCU	Heavy Conversion Unit
HE	High Explosive
Hptm	Hauptmann (Flt Lt)
IAS	Indicated Airspeed
IB	Incendiary Bomb
JG	*Jagdgeschwader* (Wing)
LWT	Lost Without Trace
Mjr	Major
'Nickel'	Leaflet raid
NFD	No further details
NFT	Night Flying Test
NJG	Nachtjagdgeschwader (Night Fighter Wing)
OBE	Order of the British Empire
Oberst	Oberst (Gp Capt)
Oblt	Oberleutnant (Fg Off)
Ofw	Oberfeldwebel (Flt Sgt)
OTU	Operational Training Unit
Plt Off	Pilot Officer
PM	Prime Minister
POW	Prisoner of War
RFU	Refresher Flying Unit
SBC	Small Bomb Container
Sgt	Sergeant
S/L	Searchlight
Sqn Ldr	Squadron Leader
Stab	*Staff* (Luftwaffe HQ unit)
T.R.	Transmitter/Receiver
TRE	Telecommunications Research Establishment
TT&G	Target Towing & Gunnery
Wg Cdr	Wing Commander
WO	Warrant Officer
Wo/AG	Wireless Operator/Air Gunner
ZG	*Zerstörergeschwader* (Destroyer Wing or Group)

Index

The Thousand Bomber Raids